The Writing on the Wall

The Writing on the Wall

Seeing the Holy Spirit in Life

JUSTIN BRENT WALLACE

foreword by Matthew Littlefield

RESOURCE *Publications* · Eugene, Oregon

THE WRITING ON THE WALL
Seeing the Holy Spirit in Life

Resource Publications
An Imprint of Wipf and Stock Publishers
199 W. 8th Ave., Suite 3
Eugene, OR 97401

www.wipfandstock.com

PAPERBACK ISBN: 979–8–3852–1351–1
HARDCOVER ISBN: 979–8–3852–1352–8
EBOOK ISBN: 979–8–3852–1353–5

VERSION NUMBER 09/12/24

The writing of this story is partly inspired by an old friend who I'd lost touch with 18 years ago, coming back into my life and me desiring to tell this old friend the full story of what happened to me and why it was so challenging and rewarding and that he would hopefully be inspired by this in his own faith walk to put even more trust in the Lord and the Holy Spirit's calling. That friend's name is Pastor Tim Lucas of the Gateway Baptist Church Main Campus at Mackenzie, Queensland, Australia; a place I attended for several years in the early 2000s and a place I returned to once again attend in 2023.

So this story is partly me, talking to Tim (with a broader audience) as I communicate this story to an old friend, who has also inspired me with his own journey from Business Honors Student to Pastor of a 5000 attender strong megachurch since our original friendship lost touch in 2005.

"You will seek me and find me when you search for me with all your heart."
— Jeremiah 29:13 (NIV)

"If you find from your own experience that something is a fact and it contradicts what some authority has written down, then you must abandon the authority and base your reasoning on your own findings."
— Leonardo Da Vinci

Contents

Foreword by Rev. Matthew Littlefield | *ix*

Acknowledgements | *xxvii*

Abbreviations | *xxviii*

Synopsis: The Writing on the Wall event | *xxix*

Introduction: Qualifying the Called | *xxxi*

Chapter 1: The Writing on the Wall or Out of the Land of Haran into the Land of Canaan | 1

Chapter 2: Returning the Apple to the Tree or Out of the Land of Canaan into the Land of Haran | 12

Chapter 3: At the House with the Writing on the Wall, the Next Day, My Reaction and the Greater Problem | 21

Chapter 4: The Gospel According to Justin | 38

Chapter 5: Confession Time and Discerning the Holy Spirit in My Life | 46

Chapter 6: Discerning the Voice of the Holy Spirit in Your Life | 53

Chapter 7: The Nature of the Holy Spirit | 72

Conclusion: Living Dangerously with the Holy Spirit | 84

Afterword: A Second Conclusion | 96

My Response to Issues Raised by the Experts | *99*

About the Author | *105*

Bibliography | *107*

Foreword

REV. MATTHEW LITTLEFIELD

DISCERNING THE VOICE OF GOD

Earlier this year Justin got together with me over coffee and asked me if I would read his upcoming book and consider even writing a foreword. He shared with me the exciting news that he had sent his book off to publishers and he had actually gotten a response and that a reputable publisher would be publishing his story. I have known Justin for many years in my capacity, first as a ministry intern and then as a pastor (though I wasn't his pastor); though our paths have diverged a bit in that time. When he asked me to read his book I was interested and thought it might be intriguing to see how his personal walk of faith had developed and because he had long been an encouragement to me I considered it a good thing to read his book and give him some constructive feedback. I am an author myself and it is vital for authors, especially those new to publishing, to be given feedback on what is good and what can be improved in their books.

When he asked me to write the foreword though, then I was a little more hesitant. Because Justin told me that he was writing a book about how to discern the voice of the Holy Spirit at work in our lives. This gave me pause because as I have known Justin for some years I knew that he was highly intelligent, deeply sensitive, incredibly talented at communicating himself, but also because of his mental health issues, something he is open about in his book, I knew that he had gotten himself into some bad situations because of his misreading of the voice of God in his life. I also knew that Justin is given to oversharing. As a friend, and someone who had ministered with him in the past, I was concerned that he would not be doing himself any favors by bearing all in a story reflecting on some of his most humiliating moments.

And you will read about some of these moments in the book. Justin is open and honest in a way that few people are. He genuinely believes that what he is writing is the truth, but he is also self-aware enough, probably more than most people, that his ability to read the situation or process the information is at times flawed. This is true for all of us to some degree, but when someone struggles with mental illness that battle to process and understand their current circumstances takes on a whole new dimension and difficulty.

And it's here that I have to unreservedly commend Justin. His book is open and honest about his struggles in this arena, and yet he also manages to show that despite his faults God is at work in his life, clinging on to him. And this truly is the kind of God we believe in and we should be thankful that we have a God like that. Because our Lord, the Lord Jesus Christ, is the kind of heavenly savior we need. Our Lord is not looking for perfect instruments, but he is looking down at the incredibly flawed human race and deciding to work with us and through us anyway to extend his kingdom in this world. Not only does our Lord Jesus Christ do this, but he does this at the behest of his heavenly Father, and the Father and Son send to us the Holy Ghost to live in us as believers and turn us into something beautiful. In a real and genuine way God takes us as malformed lumps of clay and reshapes us in the image of his son.

> "And we know that for those who love God all things work together for good, for those who are called according to his purpose. For whom he foreknew he also predestined to be conformed to the image of his Son, in order that he might be the firstborn among many brothers."[1]

This is the wonderful fruit and result of the gospel, God makes a way for us to not only be saved, but also to be transformed. You will see how God does this in Justin's life, despite his flaws, misinterpretations of the work of God and more. God is great in his mercy and wonder to us as fallen human beings. So I am being serious when I say that I commend Justin here, because he wants to show you, what God has done for many believers; transformed them by the grace of God, and worked in them and through them despite their faults.

---

1. New King James Version, *Romans 8:28-29*, www.bible.com

Be that as it may, I have serious issues with this book and they fit into three main categories: 1) Justin overshares and this can be to his own detriment, 2) His theology of how to discern the Spirit's leading I deeply disagree with, 3) His example of how to follow that voice is often to me a model of what not to do, especially if you struggle with mental illness. *I am only writing this foreword on the condition that it is published in full with its deep warning about the dangers of seeking to discern the Holy Spirit voice in the way Justin does.* I am not over-exaggerating my concern for people, especially mentally ill people, who might read this book and imitate some of its teachings and actions and get seriously hurt, or deeply regress in their mental health. So, I am going to thoroughly address these concerns now.

Firstly, the oversharing. Justin is genuine in believing that being open and raw enables him to better communicate his story. And I must admit that he is not completely wrong. His raw self-reflections often hitting the exact right self-criticism, though not always, make his book an interesting read, especially when he is telling us about some of the more dramatic points of his life. His reflection on how wrong it was to think that he was Jesus and escape from that mental ward is the correct reflection. There is nothing wrong with using some examples of our failures in life to help teach others. However, I question the wisdom of him putting this book out there for the public to read and focus on.

I know Justin has some goals for his life, outside of just being a writer, and I have counseled him that publishing these things might get in the way of him achieving these goals. To Justin's credit, he is aware of this, and I think the reader needs to be made aware of this too. What Justin is doing here is not unprecedented, many a person has published some form of tell all book, but I still question whether it is wise for someone who has struggled so deeply with mental illness to bare themselves so thoroughly. This will come with a cost. Perhaps that cost is worth it for Justin. But I believe as a pastor (I am not Justin's current pastor, and was only a trainee when we were in the same church) I have responsibility to address this. When someone struggles with mental health issues, of really any kind, public attention, recognition, or exposure can turn what is a hard battle into a frightful one.

That being said, I have no doubt that the openness of Justin's story will resonate with some people. Plenty of people struggle with mental illness, and their stories are often hidden, or pushed to the side. The reality of this world is that we are all broken instruments of one variety or another and there are a multitude of people who can probably relate to many of Justin's

experiences, struggles, victories and defeats. One thing I will keep empha-
sizing is the beauty of our God in persisting with Justin even when Justin's
actions and theology deeply rebelled against the word, and therefore will,
of God. I don't know about you but I praise God that we have such a patient
Lord who is willing to work with such broken people as we all are. But that
does not mean that Justin's example is one to follow.

Secondly, I want to address points 2) and 3) together. A book giving
advice to people on how to discern the Holy Spirit's voice is a good idea. A
book helping someone with mental illness seek to discern the Holy Spirit's
voice is a doubly good idea. In fact, I would go so far as to say that a short,
helpful and insightful book on how a mentally ill person can ground themselves in the will and wisdom of God is a necessary thing. The problem is
that Justin's book is not that. There is situations in this book and advice
given that if someone were to imitate they could die. Justin at one point
strips down and throws himself in a river, at the so-called behest of God.
At another point, believing he is Jesus incarnate, he throws himself in front
of an oncoming car, after having escaped from a mental health ward. This
is incredibly dangerous behavior. That does not mean someone could not
write about this happening in their lives and reflect on it. But the person
who does this wisely would be drawing out the principles of how this was
a bad thing, how to avoid doing this yourself, and how to identify that you
have entered into a mental health episode. (To be fair Justin does note this
about the time he thought he was Jesus.) At times Justin does reflect on how
his thinking was bad in these situations, but at other times he doesn't and
this is what makes this book concerning to me in places.

The word of God is referred to in the Scriptures as the Sword of the
Spirit. Swords, unlike some other weapons, take incredibly long, dedicated
and focused training to be able to use without cutting your own hand or
head off. If you were to pick up a sword at a medieval fair and use it to
try and do actual combat you could seriously hurt yourself. If, however,
you trained with it in a dedicated way, you would be able to use it more
effectively. I see serious danger in how Justin is encouraging people to use
the Sword of the Spirit.

Let me now address the theology. Justin is very dedicated to wanting to help train you to discern the Spirit's voice in your life. Here are two
examples of his aims:

> "I hope this book has prompted you to obey more of the spirit's
> promptings in future. No matter how crazy the prompting may

make you feel. It's only pride at times that prevents us from revealing that it might just be the Holy Spirit prompting us to start a
conversation with a stranger at church. And is that pride a good
thing? You know the answer to that."[2]

"To put it another way, this potentially controversial idea I'm talking about here is kind of like the concept of a hive mind . . . except
what I'm saying is we each have a hive spirit, living in each of us,
called the Holy Spirit. Some will heed the spirit's inclinations and
voice and find life . . . others rebel against the spirit unto death.
Indeed the unforgivable sin, seems to imply in context that it is
attributing to the Holy Spirit, evil works. Which can in the end,
only be a complete and utter tuning out of the Holy Spirit in your
mind/heart and labelling his inclinations hence as utter foolishness, so you don't follow them. So you'll miss out on the eternal
life made possible through the spirit living in us and everlasting
forgiveness through Jesus and permanently restored relationship
with God the father that was fractured in the Garden of Eden."[3]

There are at least two serious errors here. Firstly, the idea that we must
discern the Spirit's voice internally, from the other voices. Secondly, that
everyone has the Holy Spirit inside of them. The second error is easy to address, as Peter the Apostle says in Acts the Holy Spirit is only for those who
repent and are baptized, that is those who repent and believe.

"And Peter said to them, "Repent and be baptized every one of
you in the name of Jesus Christ for the forgiveness of your sins,
and you will receive the gift of the Holy Spirit. For the promise is
for you and for your children and for all who are far off, everyone
whom the Lord our God calls to himself."[4]

The promise of receiving the Holy Spirit is extended to all. But it is
only fulfilled for those who are elect, or those who trust in the Lord Jesus
Christ. This is what makes us part of the Church of God, receiving the Holy
Spirit;

"For just as the body is one and has many members, and all the
members of the body, though many, are one body, so it is with
Christ. For in one Spirit we were all baptized into one body—Jews

2. Wallace, *The Writing on the Wall*, p70
3. Wallace, *The Writing on the Wall*, p74
4. English Standard Version, *Acts 2:38–39*, www.bible.com

or Greeks, slaves or free—and all were made to drink of one Spirit."[5]

If everyone had the Holy Spirit, then everyone would be a part of the Church. But only those who believe and who are baptized by the Spirit are Christians, because being baptized by the Spirit is what makes us Christian;

> "But when the goodness and loving kindness of God our Savior appeared, he saved us, not because of works done by us in righteousness, but according to his own mercy, by the washing of regeneration and renewal of the Holy Spirit, whom he poured out on us richly through Jesus Christ our Savior."[6]

So Justin errs seriously when he says that non-believers have the Holy Spirit in them, calling out to them, seeking to lead them.

Now, there is a sense in which the Holy Spirit does convict this world, as Jesus tells us in John;

> "Nevertheless, I tell you the truth: it is to your advantage that I go away, for if I do not go away, the Helper will not come to you. But if I go, I will send him to you. And when he comes, he will convict the world concerning sin and righteousness and judgment: concerning sin, because they do not believe in me; concerning righteousness, because I go to the Father, and you will see me no longer; concerning judgment, because the ruler of this world is judged."[7]

But this is not the same as indwelling all people or being with all people. The Holy Spirit is the seal of a Christian's salvation[8], not something for all people. When someone is preached the word of God, or is reading the Bible, or in many other contexts is encountering the truth of Christ, the Holy Spirit interacts with their lives. But many people resist this and trample the grace of God, reject the truth and therefore stand condemned because of this.[9] The Holy Spirit absolutely does not dwell in non-believers. He is God and therefore dwells amongst God's people, "Or do you not know that your body is a temple of the Holy Spirit within you, whom you have from God? You are not your own, for you were bought with a price. So

5. English Standard Version, *1 Corinthians 12:12–13*, www.bible.com
6. English Standard Version, *Titus 3:4–6*, www.bible.com
7. English Standard Version, *John 16:7–11*, www.bible.com
8. New International Version, *Ephesians 1:13*, www.bible.com
9. English Standard Version, *Hebrews 10:26–31*, www.bible.com

glorify God in your body."[10] It is certainly unorthodox Christianity to say unbelievers have the Holy Spirit, as Justin himself acknowledges: "To put it another way, this potentially controversial idea I'm talking about here is kind of like the concept of a hive mind . . . except what I'm saying is we each have a hive spirit, living in each of us, called the Holy Spirit."[11] It is not just potentially controversial it is absolutely incorrect.

The other claim that you can internally discern the Spirit's voice though is much more debated in the Church, much more commonly accepted, and though perhaps not at the same level of error, practically speaking it is the far more dangerous idea, especially for the mentally ill person.

The issue here is that Justin treats discerning the Holy Spirit's voice much more like using the force, than how the Bible advises that we do this. This is common in the church. And it needs to be rebuked for many reasons, 1) it is erroneous, 2) it is dangerous, 3) in the case of a mentally ill person it can be tragic.

The question, how do you discern the voice of the Holy Spirit in your life is roughly equivalent to the question, how do you discern God's will. The answer is: you find it in the word of God. I am going to bring in something else I have written on this subject some time ago to help us here. So, let's reflect on this theology now.

HOW TO DISCERN GOD'S WILL

What do we really mean when we ask, "How do we discern the Spirit's voice in our lives?" or "What is God's will for my life?" I think when we ask this we are usually asking one of three questions? Either, "What does God want me to do?" Or "What does God have in store for my life?" or "What is God saying to me now?" I think this is what we are really asking, and these are valid questions. Part of the problem though is that Christians can ask these questions with some wrong assumptions. I think a lot of Christians genuinely believe that God is going to tell each and every person what his plan for their life is; like he did for Moses, Elijah, Jeremiah, Paul, and other biblical figures. Many Christians think he is going to come in a dream, or a prophecy, or a flash of a fiery chariot from the sky and hand you his commissioning papers for your life, or tell you who to marry, where to apply for a job, and what car to buy. Some people think, we need to listen for that still

10. English Standard Version, *1 Corinthians 16:19-20*, www.bible.com
11. Wallace, *The Writing on the Wall*, p74

small voice of the Holy Spirit whispering in our heart before we make an important life decision or even some mundane decisions. The problem is that these are wrong assumptions about how God is going to answer a valid question: "what is God's will for my life?"

Therefore, I want to try and help you have a biblical framework for how to go about seeking God's will on matters of importance in your life, to protect you from some of the theological errors I see in Justin's treatise. Let's see what the Bible says.

SEEKING GOD'S WILL IN THE OLD TESTAMENT

Let's begin by looking at how people sought God's will in the Old Testament. This is a good place to start because a lot of Christians don't realize we need to distinguish between God's work in the Old covenant, and his work in the new. So how did God speak to people in the Old Testament? 1 Samuel 28:6–7 tells us of three ways and I will add one a little later, "He inquired of the Lord, but the Lord did not answer him by dreams or Urim or prophets. Saul then said to his attendants, "Find me a woman who is a medium, so I may go and inquire of her. "There is one in Endor," they said."[12]

What is happening here is that God is refusing to speak to Saul through his usual means, so Saul goes to a witch, but the take away is this passage mentions three ways God speaks:

1. *Dreams* – we know what this is about, God spoke to Joseph, Jacob and Solomon through dreams. Joseph's dreams are famous, and have made it into Broadway plays. Solomon's are just as famous. God did come in dreams, but only rarely. In fact, there was about 12 years between when Joseph had his first dreams[13], and then in prison interpreted the baker and cupbearers' dreams[14], and another two years for Pharaoh's.[15] So even Joseph is not recorded as always having these dreams.

2. *Urim and Thummin* – This sounds like something out of Lord of the Rings, "You must consult the Urim Frodo". The Urim was used with the Thummim, and a priestly vestment, and the priest would consult God, and withdraw one of the stones. This seems to be one of the most common ways God answered the question, "What shall I do?" For example in

12. New International Version, *1 Samuel 28:6–7*, www.bible.com

13. New International Version, *Genesis 37:5*, www.bible.com

14. New International Version, *Genesis 40*, www.bible.com

15. New International Version, *Genesis 41*, www.bible.com

situations where David is deciding to go into battle.[16] Before he goes to battle he seeks the Lord's answer to the questions, should he go, or should he not. It's likely that in this situation he is actually seeking God through the Urim and Thummim.

This practice was similar to casting lots[17], something which the disciples did to choose the twelfth apostle[18], before they received the Holy Spirit[19].

3. *Prophets* – These guys are famous, starting with Moses we get heaps of prophets until Malachi. Most of the role of these guys was to address kings, leaders of Israel, including important priests, and other prophets, and sometimes the entire nation as one. There are a few exceptions, like where both Elisha and Elijah ministered to poor women who were foreigners to Israel. But nowhere in the Old Testament do we see prophets holding worship services and just dishing out to all of God's people his personal plan for their lives, or answers to who they should marry, and whether or not they should go to Uni, or start their own business. We just don't see this.

Also, these prophets could not drum up God's word in themselves. Peter tells us no prophecy was ever produced by the will of men.[20] Some only had God come a couple of times with a message, like Amos, and Jonah, some prophesied multiple times across most of their life, like Moses and Jeremiah.

4. *Theophany/Visions* – I said I add would another way, and that is Theophany's, or direct visitations of God. This is probably the most famous way. We see it with God visiting Isaiah and of course the famous burning bush visit with Moses[21], and many others. These visitations often involved angels or even the Angel of the Lord.

God came to Jeremiah and said these very famous words, "Before I formed you in the womb I knew you, before you were born I set you apart; I appointed you as a prophet to the nations."[22] Here God comes to Jeremiah and tells him what his plan for his life is, God did the same for Moses, Joseph, Isaiah and several others in the Old Testament. But never does the

16. New International Version, *1 Samuel 30:7-10*, www.bible.com
17. New International Version, *Proverbs 16:33*, www.bible.com
18. New International Version, *Acts 1*, www.bible.com
19. New International Version, *Acts 2*, www.bible.com
20. New International Version, *2 Peter: 1:21*, www.bible.com
21. New International Version, *Exodus 3*, www.bible.com
22. New International Version, *Jeremiah 1:5*, www.bible.com

Old Testament teach us that God came to every single person and told them what his plan for their life was.

I hear some people thinking. What about through his word? Remember they did not have personal Bibles in those times. Though what Scriptures did exist, in the temple of the palace, God certainly spoke through.

HOW THE NEW TESTAMENT BELIEVER SHOULD DISCERN GOD'S WILL

God still speaks in much the same way now, as he did in the Old Testament, in fact in some ways he has increased his supernatural work;

> "'In the last days, God says, I will pour out my Spirit on all people. Your sons and daughters will prophesy, your young men will see visions, your old men will dream dreams. Even on my servants, both men and women, I will pour out my Spirit in those days and they will prophesy.'"[23]

God has increased his supernatural work through the presence of his Holy Spirit in every believer. We should be seeing dreams, and visions, and prophecies in the New Testament church, and people certainly do. I do not deny that God can and does speak to people still today. But we need to ask ourselves this question? Does this mean that when it comes to making big decisions in life that we should always wait on God for a dream, a vision, a prophecy, or a direct visitation from God himself? Or try to discern the Spirit's voice in our heads or hearts?

No, because God does not promise to reveal his secret will for our lives to all of us. He actually sets out a very different method for seeking his will and making decisions for our lives. He tells us; "Do not conform to the pattern of this world, but be transformed by the renewing of your mind. Then you will be able to test and approve what God's will is — his good, pleasing and perfect will."[24] The world tells us to follow our hearts, songs tell us to follow our hearts, love stories tell us to follow our hearts. Many parts of this world will tell us to look internally to discern God's will for us, or what God is saying to us. But the Bible contradicts this.

We are told, "be transformed." We don't discern God's will for our lives by chasing after dreams, prophecies and visions, otherwise you will

23. New International Version, *Acts 2:17–18*, www.bible.com
24. New International Version, *Romans 12:2*, www.bible.com

never act. Nor do we seek his will by trying to sense it like some kind of Jedi Knight, the feelings of our heart are more often than not deceptive rather than helpful.[25] The voices we hear in our head should not be examined to see if they are our voice, a demon's voice or the Holy Spirit's voice. That is not how we discern the will of God, or the leading of the Spirit. No we do it by having our mind renewed and transformed. How do we do this? By reading God's word and saturating our minds with his truth.

If you do this "you will know his will." This means when the Bible says that we discern "the will of God", or "discern the leading of the Spirit", we are discerning what he says in his word that we can do and can't do, what we should do and what we shouldn't do. All that is good, acceptable, and perfect for us to do is revealed in Scripture. In other words, we are discerning God's revealed will, what he has written for us is, in his grace and mercy. In this we have a massive advantage over Old Testament saints because they didn't all have bibles, and most of the prophets walking around Israel were false prophets, which is the same today, but we have God's word to help.

We are not promised to know God's specific will for our lives, but we are given his revealed will and this helps us to act according to the will of God. Here are examples of how the Bible says this;

> "Finally, then, brothers, we ask and urge you in the Lord Jesus, that as you received from us how you ought to walk and to please God, just as you are doing, that you do so more and more. For you know what instructions we gave you through the Lord Jesus. For this is the will of God, your sanctification: that you abstain from sexual immorality; that each one of you know how to control his own body in holiness and honor, not in the passion of lust like the Gentiles who do not know God..."[26]

You see here how Paul is outlining the will of God for us so that we don't have to try and work it out. This is how the Holy Spirit guides us.

> "Rejoice always, pray without ceasing, give thanks in all circumstances; for this is the will of God in Christ Jesus for you. Do not quench the Spirit. Do not despise prophecies, but test everything; hold fast what is good. Abstain from every form of evil."[27]

---

25. New International Version, *Jeremiah 17:9*, www.bible.com
26. English Standard Version, *1 Thessalonians 4:1–5*, www.bible.com
27. English Standard Version, *1 Thessalonians 5:16–21*, www.bible.com

Here Paul is saying clearly what God's will for us is: rejoice, always. He does not deny God can speak through prophetic utterances, but he simply says test them. And how do you test them? Well, do they line up with God's revealed will in his word? If not you are being deceived, if yes then perhaps God has spoken to you.

> "Be subject for the Lord's sake to every human institution, whether it be to the emperor as supreme, or to governors as sent by him to punish those who do evil and to praise those who do good. For this is the will of God, that by doing good you should put to silence the ignorance of foolish people. Live as people who are free, not using your freedom as a cover-up for evil, but living as servants of God. Honor everyone. Love the brotherhood. Fear God. Honor the emperor."[28]

What is God's will here? That we do good and so silence the talk of foolish people who seek to criticize the Church and Christians.

So, if you want to hear the Holy Spirit's voice then what do you need to do? Not look within, you simply need to pick up a Bible, read it in context and listen. This is a prominent and important teaching in the Bible. This is also actually taught in Proverbs 3:5–8 where Solomon says;

> "Trust in the Lord with all your heart, and do not lean on your own understanding. In all your ways acknowledge him, and he will make straight your paths. Be not wise in your own eyes; fear the Lord, and turn away from evil. It will be healing to your flesh and refreshment to your bones."[29]

Solomon is saying the same thing here as Peter and Paul.

"Trust the Lord with all your heart, and do not lean on your own understanding"[30] is equal to "be not wise in your own eyes, fear the Lord, and turn away from evil."[31] To discern God's will, to hear the Holy Spirit's voice; we need to recognize that we are fallen people, with fallen thinking, and that our understanding is not perfect. So we must lean into God, and trust him to guide us. If you do this and " . . . in all your ways acknowledge him . . . he will make straight your paths"[32]. In all that we do we have to get

---

28. English Standard Version, *1 Peter 2:13–17*, www.bible.com
29. English Standard Version, *Proverbs 3:5–8*, www.bible.com
30. English Standard Version, *Proverbs 3:5*, www.bible.com
31. English Standard Version, *Proverbs 3:7*, www.bible.com
32. English Standard Version, *Proverbs 3:6*, www.bible.com

to know God and we will know which way to go. How do we do this? We read his word, pray for his Spirit to fill us, and we ask for wisdom which he promises to give.

And when we do this; "It will be healing to your flesh and refreshment to your bones."[33] It will be freeing. Have you ever felt the physical effects of not knowing what to do? Rather than living in fear, of not knowing what to do or what to decide, we can take what God has told us in his word and apply it to our lives and make decisions based on how we know he would have us act. And we also know that he gives us freedom, within the guidelines of his words, to make our own decisions. You don't need to try and discern the guiding of the Spirit in some force-like way. You simply need to read God's word, prayer regularly, seek godly counsel and make wise decisions. Whenever we read God's word we hear the Spirit speaking to us; "and take the helmet of salvation, and the sword of the Spirit, which is the word of God."[34] God's word has great power to transform us;

> "Let us therefore strive to enter that rest, so that no one may fall by the same sort of disobedience. For the word of God is living and active, sharper than any two-edged sword, piercing to the division of soul and of spirit, of joints and of marrow, and discerning the thoughts and intentions of the heart. And no creature is hidden from his sight, but all are naked and exposed to the eyes of him to whom we must give account."[35]

As I said above, seeking guidance from wise counsellors is important too. Don't forget this; "Where there is no guidance, a people falls, but in an abundance of counselors there is safety."[36]

What does this all look like? Let's get really practical:

Seeking the Spirit's leading on marriage? Look at what the Bible says about marriage: do not be unequally yoked[37], men you need to provide, etc, etc.

Seeking the Spirit's leading on your profession? Look at what the Bible says: whatever you do, do it for the glory of God.[38]

---

33. English Standard Version, *Proverbs 3:8*, www.bible.com

34. English Standard Version, *Ephesians 6:17*, www.bible.com

35. English Standard Version, *Hebrews 4:11–12*, www.bible.com

36. English Standard Version, *Proverbs 11:14*, www.bible.com

37. New International Version, *2 Corinthians 6:14*, www.bible.com

38. New International Version, *1 Corinthians 10:31*, www.bible.com

Seeking the Spirit's leading on friends? Look at what the Bible says: don't be in the company of fools.[39]

Seeking the Spirit's voice on where to go to Church? Look at what the Bible says: engage in a church that teaches God's word, where they love one another, and seek to be a light to the world.[40]

Seeking the Spirit's voice on how to use your money? Look at what the Bible says: be generous, give, and be a good steward.[41]

God wants us to use our mind, a mind that we have worked hard to fill with the knowledge of him, and he wants our hearts to desire what he would desire, and then he wants us to act. If he decides to come to you in a more specific and supernatural way then that is completely at his choosing. But considering what the people went through who God came to in the Bible, you may not want to crave that too much.

LED BY THE SPIRIT?

What the Bible says about being led by the Spirit is often misunderstood by many Christians as well. They see this and they think, "Aha, this is where I need to work out what the Spirit's voice is saying to me." Pastors who teach this are incredibly irresponsible and having grown up in Pentecostal churches one of the flaws I saw in that denomination (I am not picking on them, every denomination has its issues/are imperfect) is that a lot of mentally unwell, or mentally fragile people were incredibly attracted to that theology of seeking God's voice because it affirmed their highly subjective way of living their lives and following God. To this day I believe that charismatic Baptists and Pentecostals which teach people to "listen for the still small voice[42] of the Spirit" are doing incredible damage, but especially to mentally ill people.

Being led by the Spirit is about having your desires prompting you to live righteously, not sinfully. Paul is clear about this. For instance Romans 8 says this;

> "So then, brothers, we are debtors, not to the flesh, to live accord-
> ing to the flesh. For if you live according to the flesh you will die,

---

39. New International Version, *Proverbs 14:7*, www.bible.com

40. New International Version, *2 Corinthians 4:6*, www.bible.com

41. New International Version, *1 Timothy 6:18*, www.bible.com

42. New International Version, *1 Kings 19:12*, www.bible.com

but if by the Spirit you put to death the deeds of the body, you will live. For all who are led by the Spirit of God are sons of God. For you did not receive the spirit of slavery to fall back into fear, but you have received the Spirit of adoption as sons, by whom we cry, "Abba! Father!" The Spirit himself bears witness with our spirit that we are children of God, and if children, then heirs—heirs of God and fellow heirs with Christ, provided we suffer with him in order that we may also be glorified with him."[43]

There is nothing in here about having to try and hear the voice of the Holy Spirit. Paul simply means that the Spirit prompts us to live righteously and the flesh prompts us to sin, follow the leading of the Spirit to do what is right, not the flesh. The Spirit prompts us to cry out in praise to God, calling him father, we do not need to try and listen for its voice.

As clear as this is in Romans, Paul makes it even more clear in Galatians;

"But I say, walk by the Spirit, and you will not gratify the desires of the flesh. For the desires of the flesh are against the Spirit, and the desires of the Spirit are against the flesh, for these are opposed to each other, to keep you from doing the things you want to do. But if you are led by the Spirit, you are not under the law. Now the works of the flesh are evident: sexual immorality, impurity, sensuality, idolatry, sorcery, enmity, strife, jealousy, fits of anger, rivalries, dissensions, divisions, envy, drunkenness, orgies, and things like these. I warn you, as I warned you before, that those who do such things will not inherit the kingdom of God. But the fruit of the Spirit is love, joy, peace, patience, kindness, goodness, faithfulness, gentleness, self-control; against such things there is no law. And those who belong to Christ Jesus have crucified the flesh with its passions and desires. If we live by the Spirit, let us also keep in step with the Spirit. Let us not become conceited, provoking one another, envying one another."[44]

Again there is nothing here about listening for the still quiet voice of God to be led by the Spirit. The fruit of the Spirit's leading is righteous living, the fruit of the flesh is sin. If you want to be led by the Spirit read God's word, and do not override your conscience to sin. You hear the Spirit's voice in his word and you follow his leading by feeding the righteous impulses of the Spirit in your life.

43. English Standard Version, *Romans 8:12–17*, www.bible.com
44. English Standard Version, *Galatians 5:16–26*, www.bible.com

LET'S APPLY THIS

So, now we need to apply this in light of God's word and Justin's book. There are several instances where Justin breaks the will of God because he believes he is being told to do so. Take the example of buying a porn magazine in the airport. This is engaging in sexual immorality. So it is very simple, how do we determine this is the voice of God or not? Does it agree with God's word? No. Therefore, it is not the Holy Spirit. The same applies to stripping naked and getting in the river. Or breaking out of the mental ward and getting in front of a moving car. These actions break many different commands of God, therefore they are against God's word and therefore his will and are not the voice of the Spirit.

But we have a difficulty here, what about things God's word does not exactly address, like going to New Zealand? Well, especially if you are mentally ill, you need to follow the advice from above.

Compare what you think is the Spirit's voice to God's word. If you have bills, commitments, a job, etc, you are not to just leave such things, you have a responsibility to fulfill your commitments, you also have a responsibility to live wisely. But, if you are mentally ill and know you have a tendency to hear voices, you need to follow this framework mentioned above even more than most people. Let me summarize it again: a) do not lean on your own understanding[45], b) trust God and that his word will guide you, c) speak to wise counsellors who can speak to your behavior, d) submit yourself to their counsel knowing that even more than the average person you cannot trust your own discernment. This is humbling, it is hard. But it is vitally necessary. The more you deal with mental illness, the more you will think some kind of mental high or low is the result of a spiritual awakening, knowledge or experience, when it is more likely just the result of not enough sleep, or some other health issue. You need to be extra humble in restraining your actions, doubting yourself, or not leaning on your own understanding. Your life may depend on it. Others lives may depend on it.

Everyone needs to recognize their thinking is flawed and that they need wise counsel, we all need this. But some of us need to rely on it even more, that includes those who have hurt themselves or others in the past, or know they have mental health issues.

If you know that you have a tendency to get into spiritual highs and end up in a mental ward, you need to protect yourself by surrounding

45. English Standard Version, *Proverbs 3:5*, www.bible.com

yourself with wise support and you need to recognize that you often can't trust yourself. All of us will lead ourselves astray from time to time. But the mentally ill person has this struggle in a multitude of extra ways. It is tragic, unfair, and even a cruel reality, but it is a reality. Protect yourself, and never look inward for guidance.

I love Justin, he is a good man. I think his journey has lessons in it for all of us. I just think his book takes the wrong lessons. You should not listen to his theology or examples, but listen to his struggles and recognize that in Justin is a good man who has been dealt a bad hand in life with an ongoing struggle. This life can be hard, especially when you can't trust your own discernment. But it can still be navigated with joy. And praise God that we serve a God, the God Justin lifts up, who is gracious and compassionate to sinners like us, as long as we are humble; "Good and upright is the Lord; therefore he instructs sinners in the way. He leads the humble in what is right, and teaches the humble his way."[46]

— Reverend Matthew Littlefield,
Brisbane, Australia, April 2024

46. English Standard Version, *Psalms 25:8–9*, www.bible.com

Acknowledgements

Several people have assisted me in the production of this book and I would like to acknowledge them.

The production team at WIPF and Stock/Resource Publications, My oldest friend Lotawai Otukolo and his father Honi Otukolo, Matthew Littlefield, Garry Toms, Justin Dunford, Troy Stoikovski and Tim Lucas.

Abbreviations

Please note as it is hoped many first time spiritual readers will pick up this book, I have decided not to abbreviate the names of scriptural books for easy reference.

Synopsis
The Writing on the Wall event

This is a True Story about a real world miraculous event proving God Exists that only occurred because of my submission to listening to and discerning clearly the voice of the Holy Spirit.

For this synopsis I've included simply the brief summary of the main story and how I in general introduce it to people/strangers in person; the greater details, reaction and exploration of the issues is what concerns the larger story.

"How do I know God exists?"

I don't have faith in God anymore. I have knowledge of him. Like knowing the sun came up in the sky today because you can see it and feel it.

This happened because of my writing on the wall experience I had in Christchurch. Would you like to hear it? It'll just take a minute of your time to hear. (Sure)

One night in Brisbane, Australia in March 2007, I was reading the bible and I felt a strong sense from the Holy Spirit to travel to Christchurch, New Zealand where I had never been before.

The next morning I flew there and after wandering around for a day and a half, I stopped in front of a suburban street like any other, and in a bit of righteous anger, I asked God why had he brought me here? What was the point?

Then I felt the Holy Spirit in my mind answer my righteous anger. "Because, you've trusted and obeyed me, I'm going to give you what you want most right now."

Immediately riches passed through my mind, before realizing that what I wanted most right now, was a safe place to sleep for the night. I was tired and weary.

"All right," the Holy Spirit said, "Turn down the driveway of this house you're nearest to, you'll find the back door unlocked and you can sleep there for the night."

"Whoa," I replied, "I'm not comfortable breaking and entering. I've never done that before!"

"What if you had the owner's permission, would that make you comfortable?"

"I don't understand."

"I've put you to the test in coming this far . . . just put me to the test now. Try the backdoor of the house. It will be unlocked."

"All right Lord, I've come this far, I'll put you to the test."

And not only did I find the back door unlocked and the house empty but I also found painted in large red writing on the rear wall of the house *"We the owners have gone away and if you read this you have our permission to stay as long as you like."*

Conclusion:

So, getting the prophecy immediately fulfilled for me, put the final nail in the coffin proving God exists. I had travelled over four thousand miles . . . walked aimlessly for two days . . . to arrive at the one place on earth prepared in advance for my arrival. The odds of all that taking place . . . with no God . . . are astronomical. . .

It is also an immediate fulfillment/proof of Psalms 139:4 "Before a word is on my tongue, you, Lord, know it completely."[47]

This book goes on to explore the details, my reactions and make a comment on what you need to do for how you too can accurately discern the holy spirit speaking to you and better see his presence in your life.

---

47. New International Version, *Psalms 139:4*, www.bible.com

Introduction

Qualifying the Called

"'Return home and tell how much God has done for you.' So the man went away and told all over town how much Jesus had done for him."[48] — Luke 8:39

Firstly, a little about me. I am a 49 year old single man from Brisbane, Australia living with my beloved cat, Terry. I was raised in the Baptist church. Baptized at 16; Married at 21; Divorced at 26. I'm a former high school drama, history and english teacher, former counsellor and a current filmmaker, producer, director, writer and editor. I also have a Bachelor of Arts in Communication, Drama and History, a Graduate Diploma in Counseling and a Masters of Business in Marketing. (I will reveal more relevant details about me as the story is revealed.)

In March 2007, I experienced an event in Christchurch, New Zealand, so unlikely to have happened that I call it a modern day miracle in the like of Paul's journey to Damascus[49], encountering Jesus (though mine was encountering undeniable proof of the Holy Spirit living in me) and also reminiscent of vindication for Abraham being called out of the land of Ur/ Haran, into the land of Canaan[50], his faith test with Isaac[51] and having his faith credited to him as righteousness[52].

---

48. New International Version, *Luke 8:39*, www.bible.com
49. New International Version, *Acts 9:1–8*, www.bible.com
50. New International Version, *Genesis 12:1*, www.bible.com
51. New International Version, *Genesis 22:1–18*, www.bible.com
52. New International Version, *Genesis 15:6*, www.bible.com

This event had a massive effect on my spiritual life and filtered through every area of my life as I struggled to come to grips with what had happened. Struggled to make sense of the world and my faith and what had changed for me after this.

This is my autobiographical retelling of the event, its effect on me, the greater context and how I struggled and even rebelled against God's truth revealed unarguably to me at the time, fell into sin/twisted theology and needed every bit of faith I had, to overcome my stumbling blocks and return to God with accurate theology, like the prodigal son; "when he came to his senses."[53]

It is a story of faith, obedience, vindication, rebellion, restoration, sanctification and justification that I believe will inspire and challenge the faith journey of all people regardless of their faith background who become aware of this and hence I believe that what I have to say, has relevance for your own journey and how you live your life subsequently in practice as a result of reading this story about me as well as how you detect the Holy Spirit's presence and the influence you allow the Holy Spirit to have on your own life.

Now; I am at a place where like the Demon possessed man healed by Jesus[54]; I am ready to tell the full story of what happened and my encounter with God.

I also believe God doesn't exactly call the qualified to be his witnesses . . . he qualifies those he calls. You can study all the theology the bible offers surrounding the Holy Spirit to your heart's content and not be at all an expert on discerning the Holy Spirit's inner voice inside your mind from your own thoughts/inner voice. Nothing I say, disputes what is in the bible theologically . . . but what I do say shows a proven scientific method of testing and quantifying the results to show how to determine and prove systematically that the inner voice speaking to me was in fact, the Holy Spirit — and hence, I had proof of God's existence, and hence, thus, those directions ought to be listened to and hence "his" directions should ideally be followed like scripture. And the reward for so doing . . . is the reward of knowing God and knowing he exists. And that is my apologetic/defence of the faith approach in this book. I know God exists because I've experienced unarguable proof of him communicating to me directly in my mind. As opposed to where I once was someone, before the events detailed in this story, who simply believed

53. New International Version, *Luke 15:17*, www.bible.com
54. New International Version, *Luke 8:39*, www.bible.com

in God by faith alone and believed in him because of the truth I felt I had previously encountered from the bible. I believe God gives of himself . . . to those who seek and submit to him. And he gave me proof of his existence — that I intend to fully explore and share here.

To this end therefore, this entire story also represents what qualifies me as a leading expert on discerning/seeing the Holy Spirit in life; as well as proves I have the calling to make what I consider to be expert comments on how you too can discern the Holy Spirit; and indeed make the steps of faith, obedience, and submission required to submit to the spirit's calling in your own daily life; and finally to detect the difference between what may be your own voice in your head and what I am in fact proving, scientifically, in this entire book to co-exist in your mind — the voice of the Holy Spirit.

Your question "What would he know about detecting the Holy Spirit?" is answered directly in this story as I prove that what occurred in my life stories related here only came about because I was correctly detecting/ deducing and listening to the Holy Spirit and I dared to put into action the discernment I was showing. And as someone who has proven he is an expert on discerning the Holy Spirit — that forms my qualifications to make expert comments on what you need to do in order to effectively do the same and hence thus receive proof of God both that he exists and that he cares to work in your life; so much so that he is directly speaking to you in your own head from time to time.

"Dear friends, do not believe every spirit, but test the spirits to see whether they are from God, because many false prophets have gone out into the world."[55]

I will go on to show that I tested the Holy Spirit's advice — and definitively proved by the results of this testing that the advice came from him and not myself.

This is why I believe in the existence of God — from personally encountering and discerning his voice of his Holy Spirit speaking inside me.

So, you've read my "synopsis of the event" and still dare to doubt that I have heard his voice speaking to me?

Then the full story I'm about to share will undoubtedly blow you away and make you a believer.

And yes, that is a challenge issued and I hope accepted!

I truly hope this leaves you more inspired to submit yourself to the Holy Spirit's voice speaking inside you. If my story can help you detect

55. New International Version, *1 John 4:1*, www.bible.com

better and listen more to his guidance and see the incredible rewards and value in that; then I have done my job.

Praise God! Not me however, for everything I know is because of God's gracious blessing that followed my total commitment and submission to him.

Galatians 5:16 says "If you are guided by the spirit, you won't obey your selfish desires."[56]

Oh, if only I was always purely obedient and submissive to the truth in that verse! When I have been guided by the Holy Spirit; has been the only way I've achieved success/self-control over my own at times harmful sinful practices and desires and when I have not been submissive . . . has been when I've gotten myself into trouble! This is why this book is so important and making/emphasizing why it is so important to discern the voice of the Holy Spirit in life! Only when we do detect/discern clearly the voice of the Holy Spirit and importantly obey/submit to that — can we truly walk deeper down the path of sanctification towards genuine holiness and pleasing God.[57] Spiritual meat![58] As opposed to the spiritual milk, first baby steps into faith, of a justification by faith alone gospel.[59]

So I hope what I say here inspires you to trust the Holy Spirit inside you more in practice.

However; a word of warning. Note that even though the stories and observations I am about to share reveal my full commitment to seeing the Holy Spirit everywhere in life and listening to the Holy Spirit and what God may be saying to me above all . . . it is still important to exercise *some* discernment and not just be naive and over-eager as a result to enact every little prompting that you might *feel* is coming from the Holy Spirit. Test the spirit/message and ideally wait for proof from God in some way if possible before acting out those urges. I do acknowledge however that sometimes action must precede proof. I had to trust and obey the Holy Spirit before finding proof that that command came from God in finding the writing on the wall. Nevertheless, I hope you are all encouraged that my testing has resulted in the fruits and reward of God I received that my story reveals. But please don't just naively and eagerly obey every impulse you *might* have that you feel *could* be coming from the Holy Spirit without appropriate testing. I

56. Contemporary English Version, *Galatians 5:16*, www.bible.com
57. New International Version, *Hebrews 11:6*, www.bible.com
58. New International Version, *Hebrews 5:12*, www.bible.com
59. New International Version, *Romans 2:8*, www.bible.com

am not encouraging you to do that as a first reaction at all. For one thing, I hope you realize, the Holy Spirit will never direct you to sin.

Without appropriate testing of what *may* be the Holy Spirit's guidance occurring in your mind, you will simply be like an infant "tossed back and forth by the waves, and blown here and there by every wind of teaching and by the cunning and craftiness of people in their deceitful scheming."[60]

60. New International Version, *Ephesians 4:14*, www.bible.com

Chapter 1

The Writing on the Wall or Out of the Land of Haran into the Land of Canaan

"For you will seek me and find me, when you search for me with all your heart."[1]
— Jeremiah 29:13

THE FEEDING OF THE 5000

Before I get to the main event of my writing on the wall experience as I call it in Christchurch, New Zealand in March 2007, undoubtedly the most significant faith event in my life, the likelihood of it occurring, I call a major miracle — I would like to challenge Tim (and other potential pastors who might read this) with a possible sermon topic. (It is relevant to where I am going with my story — but also stands on its own.)

Let me ask you, the reader, a question. Jesus' feeding of the 5000 miracle.[2] Who was it for?

Was it for the 5000 people who merely ate a meal they didn't pay for and had very little idea of how it came to them? I mean, they all simply ate food presented to them didn't they, and in all likelihood, had little idea of the 'miracle of multiplication' that had just taken place.

So was it for the Disciples then? To bolster their faith and encourage them to put even more faith in Jesus and God — that might well one day be required of them when the good times were gone and only persecution and

1. New International Version, *Jeremiah 29:13*, www.bible.com
2. New International Version, *Luke 9:12–17*, www.bible.com

a hard martyred death was likely all that awaited other than their memory of such a stupendous event?

I mean, they realized that Jesus' source materials for the miracle were a mere five loaves of bread and a couple of fish. Impossible to use such physical matter to fill the stomachs of 5000 people. They became unarguably aware of the miraculous nature of the event, if they hadn't already suspected during of course, when they gathered twelve basketfuls of leftovers . . . far more than the source. Surely, they would have wondered at God and marveled at the messiah before them, who had such faith in God . . . that God heard his prayer and enabled the miracle of multiplication to take place, for the reasons God wanted it to happen.

The disciples would have been awestruck. They would have been unable to live a life . . . where accepting "normal" would still be "normal." They knew God existed and knew God would be in absolute control and despite the limits imposed on man . . . they knew God wasn't limited in the same way. If God wanted to take two fish and feed 5000 with them . . . God would do it. But it had to be God at work. Scientifically. And not man.

Surely, this is a major reason why God allowed this event to happen. These were men who would prove crucial in the formation of the early church and its spread throughout Israel and on into the larger gentile world.

But I would argue, it is not for their faith journey alone . . . that God allowed this miracle to take place. It is also for the hearers of the miracle and the effects that hearing of this miracle from a trusted source; the disciples in this instance, would have on the hearer's own lives. The very challenge that hearing of a miracle presents to your life and faith journey . . . even though you didn't actually experience that miracle.

So, it is not in the end, for those who got the miracle, nor for the faith journey alone of the disciples who realized a miracle had taken place but for you, ultimately, the reader/hearer of the event that is why the miracle took place — as well as God's glory of course.

However, as is the case with all "tellings of events" . . . you didn't experience it and can only weigh its virtues, based on what you know of the character of the teller and the likelihood of that teller being honest. Many "tall stories", furphies if you will, exist now in the age of misinformation.

And it is part of me wanting to tell the full story, to encourage you to trust that what I tell you in a rather short story simplified into a few hundred words in the synopsis; actually took place, that I am going to reveal my motives in full, pure I tell you, as well as all the details required to prove to you that I am a trusted messenger and need not be shot down because you don't know me and don't trust me. I want to let you get to know me and help you trust me and trust God by extension that what took place, actually happened as well as take my advice that I give later seriously regarding what you need to do in order to effectively detect, discern, and heed the Holy Spirit's voice more in your own life.

But in order to cease whetting your appetite, I will tell the story in full now, with all relevant details. In the process, I will tell you also more facts about me which I hope will help build your trust in me and hence, agree with my conclusions. Then you will know me; and like I do, praise God and hopefully be encouraged to put your trust in him/Jesus/the Holy Spirit even more and simply follow him; when he says go, go. When the Holy Spirit says jump, jump. And when he says stop, stop.

I have been on a journey of wisdom and discernment since and all of that has been needed to teach me all the discernment I needed to successfully apply the lessons the Holy Spirit has been teaching me, when under my own limited understanding, I fell into poor theology/sinful practices . . . and hence bring me back fully to the Lord in complete submission . . . when I surprisingly, fell away (into sin — but not from my faith in God/Jesus/the Holy Spirit) for a time after the event . . . just like Jesus would say to the disciples on the night he was betrayed that they would soon all fall away on account of him . . .[3]

Let me tell you, that I really identify having experienced my miracle, with the wide range of feelings and events such an experience leaves you with. And I hope you finish my autobiographical re-telling and subsequent analysis and don't just stop after the next few pages after I've described the detail concerned with the most significant event thus far in my life.

IN BRISBANE, MARCH 2007

Now to the event . . . to skip forward in my life story to start like Star Wars . . . in the middle of it . . . part four if you will . . .

In March 2007, at the age of 32, I was reading my bible one night in the outer suburbs of Brisbane, Queensland, Australia. While, I didn't use the actual words 'guide me' at the time, I was essentially seeking the Lord's guidance with all my heart and *completely* open to obeying him, wherever that guidance may lead.

3. New International Version, *Mark 14:27*, www.bible.com

While I was reading a passage, I cannot even remember which passage, I felt this sudden sense from the Holy Spirit to travel to Christchurch, New Zealand as God had named the place for his reasons "Christ" "Church". That there was some deeper lesson he wanted to teach me in going there and it had been named thus just for this purpose at least (if not for other reasons — who says God allows names for just one reason?).

So, not having any immediate plans to conflict with this idea, I boldly obeyed and went the next day, bought a plane ticket, and flew direct from Brisbane to Christchurch.

I liken it, in the aftermath, to Abraham being called out of the land of Haran to go to the land of Canaan.[4]

It was a suggestion that didn't make logical sense. What awaited me there? I had no idea. I had never been to Christchurch. But I felt the call had come from God . . . so, I swallowed my doubts and crucially, dared to obey . . . and in a sense, scientifically, put God to the test too. Would he have a point in my life for asking me to travel there? I doubted it . . . but I was willing to go, conduct an experiment, and gauge the results; so I went.

IN CHRISTCHURCH, THE NEXT DAY

Anyway, I arrived in Christchurch, New Zealand, later the next morning/afternoon their time and my luggage went to Melbourne, Australia. Lol. Apparently, God didn't want me to be encumbered. But I did have a trench coat and a small backpack of hand luggage.

Security even pulled me at N.Z. Customs when they realized my luggage had gone to Melbourne after I complained to the airline that my luggage hadn't appeared. They suspected something unusual. I was interviewed for an hour before being let go.

I didn't have a great deal of money at that point — yes, the trip cost me most of my savings . . . I was unemployed at that point and only receiving social unemployment benefits. So when I arrived in Christchurch, Customs Officers investigating my missing luggage wanted to know why I had so little money, and had arrived on a one way ticket.

I told them I was considering moving here, true "from a certain point of view," thanks Obi-Wan Kenobi[5] — and I wanted to look around. I wasn't sure. I felt if I told them, I flew here on a whim, simply because I felt the

4. New International Version, *Genesis 12:1*, www.bible.com
5. Marquand, *Return of the Jedi*

4

spirit of God urge me to fly here in my head; (not an audible voice . . . but a still small inner/thought like voice/impression) that they would call the mental hospital, admit me for being insane, and/or deport me straight away.

However, they decided to let me go, so I left the airport and walked towards the city centre, following street signs. Remember, I didn't have much money to spare and wanted to save it in case a situation required that I absolutely must spend it. So no taxi or bus fare.

I must've walked for hours before eventually finding myself in the city. By this time, it was 9pm or so and many restaurants were shut.

Oh, I should back up a bit here too and say, that I arrived in NZ with only my passport, and 94 dollars cash in my wallet.

For some reason, I felt God call me to come to Christchurch, without a debit card, driver's license or any other memory of my true identity of being Justin Brent Wallace.

In the aftermath of this calling, I threw my license and credit card into a bin at the airport in Brisbane, and merely kept my passport which I knew would be required to get through customs in New Zealand.

When I left the airport, I felt the time was right to throw my passport out. So it went into a bin.

Remember I told you about an extraordinary series of unlikely events occurring/preceding this miracle; such steps were also necessary to help set the scene, that I was not going to meet God as Justin Brent Wallace . . . I would have to meet him, metaphorically, as someone else . . . Justin was a sinner and unworthy of meeting God in any way . . . and Justin had to disappear as much as possible . . . me being ready and willing, and totally obedient to leave my 'self', and identity behind in order for God to consider revealing himself to me as he did — which I am getting to.

To that end, I will now reveal that I had a porn magazine in my backpack, and little else, though there was a half eaten piece of chicken (more on the chicken later) wrapped in a packet.

Why a porn magazine? Well, let's just say, that at the airport while I was waiting for my flight to open luggage check in, I felt the voice of God urge me again to go to the nearby Newsagent and do something daring and seemingly counter-intuitive.

"Buy a porn magazine and start reading it openly in public in the public lounge."

Now, I had not bought a porn magazine in years . . . that part of me, those urges and desires, I had long thought to be under control . . . but just as I was flying direct from Brisbane to Christchurch on a whim, this whim too, I felt was important. So I bought the magazine and left it open in front of me on a centerfold. At that point, there were no nefarious/urges/motivations regarding that magazine in its purchase. My motives were pure. I was merely open to seeing how and what God's point for it might be in my purchasing it.

Then I looked up from the couch I was sitting on and on the couch next to me, was the face of the woman on the centerfold. She seemed curious as to why I had the magazine opened at that time and in such a daring public place.

We began a conversation. That was rather spiritual in nature. She seemed to be testing me. She was surprised that I was traveling to Christchurch on a whim/message from God the night before. She was in transit, traveling somewhere and meeting friends at the airport.

Soon, it came time for me to load my ill-fated luggage. This lady, still unnamed, we had not exchanged names, walked with me. I deposited my luggage at the check in counter and then hugged her goodbye. She then kissed me and we kissed quite passionately for a few moments.

I then said, I was open to staying longer, missing my flight and getting to know her better. She encouraged me to take my flight. So I did.

I have often thought back to this rather strange event, preceding my miracle, and considered all sorts of meanings around this. Was she an angel I was entertaining unaware? Was she the devil himself, come to test my faith in this rather strange trial of the Holy Spirit/scientific test I was undertaking with God? Was there a greater spiritual battle/bargain taking place . . . a la, the story of Job . . . where God presented Job to Satan and a test of faith was authorized;[6] e.g., the test might've been could the Holy Spirit alone lead me to the writing on the wall? Was she really the woman on the pages of the magazine in front of me? What a strange coincidence (I also don't believe in coincidence) that was? Or did she merely carry an unexpectedly large amount of coincidental (!) resemblance to the girl in the images and was merely a young, blond, sexy woman half a dozen years or so younger than me by appearance . . . with yes, a slightly Swedish english accent, who said she came from Sweden and had done some photo shoots? (Yes she admitted to that.)

6. New International Version, *Job 1:6–12*, www.bible.com

Now, let's move forward to where I left the story at my arrival on foot in the city area of Christchurch . . .

All the shops were shutting and I felt God telling me to find somewhere out of the cold night air. March in Christchurch, deep in the southern hemisphere is still quite cold compared to a warm city much further north in the hemisphere like Brisbane at that time of year.

The only place open, I found, was the Casino. So I went in, got out of the night air and spent a few hours wandering through the games rooms, the bars and even sitting on a few couches and considering my predicament. The strange events seemingly taking place all around me and to me. It had been a fascinating journey so far . . . but did God have a real point to this? A real vindication for me, in walking this journey? (He did.) I didn't know but couldn't wait to find out.

I munched from time to time, during the 8 hours or so spent in the casino, casually, on a piece of chicken bought at the Brisbane airport (why I had $94 on me, now, not a hundred actually.) That little half-eaten piece of chicken, was then put back in its packet . . . and I ate only that, for my first three days in Christchurch; including the aftermath of the miracle at the writing on the wall. Was it too multiplied by God, like he multiplied the fish during the miracle of the 5000?[7] I don't know. Allow me to merely present the facts. A half chicken pack, lasted me three days and 25 short munching meals during that time and each time, I started eating hungry and stopped eating when my stomach felt full. (And no, that's not my spectacular miracle . . . that's merely an hors-d'oeuvre)

The chicken was yet another step on this strange journey, which one could also liken perhaps to Homer's Odyssey[8] — or a form of an Emmaus walk[9] — I suppose at this point.

WANDERING THE STREETS, THE FOLLOWING DAY

Anyway, when there was light outside, I left the casino, keeping my trench coat wrapped warmly about myself, and walked through the cold early pre-dawn streets of the city at random, and feeling the urge, left the city, and began to walk down a main thoroughfare to explore the suburban streets.

7. New International Version, *Mark 6:32–44*, www.bible.com

8. Homer, *Odyssey*

9. Unknown, *What is the Walk to Emmaus?*, www.gotquestions.org/Walk-to-Emmaus.html

I started making random turns down side streets. Stopped around midday in a children's park with a playground, rested on a park bench and had a bit of chicken again and filled up my water bottle. Before resuming my walk once more.

After doing this for a number of hours, walking down side streets. The sun set and I kept walking, and walking . . .

Eventually around midnight (I had thrown my mobile phone away at the Brisbane airport too so had no means of assessing the correct time), I stopped in a suburban street like any other and in front of a house like any other and thought to myself, "God, you know what, I've been pretty obedient on this journey. What is your point in sending me here?"

I actually felt a bit of righteous anger in me build at this point amongst all other conflicting emotions . . . as if this was actually his fault and not mine and if he didn't answer me, then all this whole journey had been but a figment of my imagination that he had sent me here; that it hadn't been God sending me on this journey . . . it had merely been my own and my naive ignorance and naive faith in him and naive belief that God could actually speak to me in such a way inside my head and guide me . . . Was I wasting my time? Was my faith in him misplaced? Was I an absolute idiot and had I lost all my mental marbles completely?

No doubt to some of you right now, that is what you're thinking about me for even going on this journey as I've explained it thus far.

Then, put simply, in simple terms with only a few extra details added, as I've explained it to several people in person in the years since; I felt the voice of God/the Holy Spirit inside me, calmly respond to my righteous anger at him.

"Because you've obeyed me in doing your best to leave Justin Wallace behind, and come to Christchurch, I'm going to give you what you want most right now."

Immediately riches passed through my mind before quickly being replaced by this sense of how tired, weary and yea, even cold I was feeling on the streets at night.

"Lord what I really want most right now is a safe, warm place where I can sleep tonight. I'm completely lost in the suburbs. I'm nowhere near a motel and feel completely tired and weary as if I could just fall asleep right here. But everywhere I see are strange houses where none will welcome me if I go knocking. Yet if you ask me to knock on a door I will."

Then I felt the Lord reply to me in my heart/mind/soul:

"I will ask you to go down the driveway of the house you are closest too. You will find the back door unlocked, the house empty and you can go sleep in peace in there tonight."

Petra's " . . . Walk by faith and not by sight"[10] song (and all that . . . circa the bible quote[11]) is my current random song selection playing on my phone (I have several thousand songs on my phone) at a rather apt (coincidental/not coincidental) time as I write this on Monday night, the eleventh, December, 2023, all these years later. Never a more apt song for a moment like this.

"Lord," I protested, "I'm not comfortable breaking and entering. I've never done that before."

"I put you to the test," I felt the Lord reply to me in my mind, "Now put me to the test one last time and learn for sure, whether it's been me guiding you or you guiding you. I know you're not comfortable entering without permission. What if you had the owner's permission?"

"I don't understand," I replied. "But if I had their permission, then yes, that would be ok."

"You will soon understand," the Holy Spirit replied. "Will you at least go down the driveway, and find out if the back door is unlocked? Is that enough for you to trust me that far?"

"All right Lord, I've come this far . . . I will try the back door and see if it is unlocked and take it as a sign that you have been leading me all along if it is . . . and if it's not . . . well, I'll come to my senses and write off this whole experience as a lesson learned in not trusting the still small voice in my head and only make sane decisions from now on."

NOW THE MIRACLE SIMPLY PUT AS THE WRITING ON THE WALL

Not only did I find the house unlocked, and the house empty, and spent the night there, but I saw painted in large red writing on the rear wall of the house; "*We the owners have gone away and if you read this you have our permission to stay as long as you like.*"

Wordy Words written on a fibro rear wall of an aging house that are burned on my brain like fire even now some 16 years later.

Yes, I slept the night away inside.

10. Petra, *Not by Sight*
11. Revised Standard Version, *2 Corinthians 5:7*, www.bible.com

What are the chances of me, having a 30 second conversation with God in front of a random house, after traveling for some 40 hours, and wandering past thousands of houses since I left my house in Brisbane, of finding the house with the writing on the wall on it's rear wall? Unable to be viewed from the street?

Where I argued with the Holy Spirit, immediately before going down that driveway and he told me the house's back door would be unlocked and be empty . . . and I would get permission to stay the night there . . . and then finding that place and suggestion and prophecy immediately fulfilled? What are the chances? About one in 4 billion I think given how many buildings there are in the world . . . I've also in my entire life, never tried a back door of anyone's house before . . . And first time, this happens!

If that's not a real world miracle in practice, I don't know what is.

I would also say God has shown me how he works in us when we "walk by faith not by sight"[12] . . . to truly see his wonders . . . his glory . . . to truly encounter him and his majesty. By human terms . . . foolishness . . . one decision I made after another . . . but God delights to show the foolishness of man is the wisdom of God.[13]

You see miracles leave you in no doubt God exists. (All the atheist/ other religion and agnostic arguments melt away into utter insignificance and ridiculousness when they occur.) So since that moment . . . since my miracle of walking by faith being vindicated by my sight of the writing on the wall . . . The scientific test I/we conducted that proved it was the Holy Spirit guiding me . . . I have felt that it wasn't just for me alone, that God granted me this experience.

Like the miracle of the feeding of the 5000 . . . it was for those who will hear about it . . . and be more inspired as a result to listen to their own inner still small voice . . . the still small voice of God the Holy Spirit . . . gently leading them to greater and greater faith and knowledge of him.

Now, I also wasn't seeking to put God to the test when I was reading the bible that night in Brisbane (until the random thought occurred about Christchurch's name — then, it felt as if I had his permission to put him to the test) . . . And I had no idea of the incredible journey and vindication for it for me that would take place just 48 hours later.

I also wasn't like the Jews in Jesus' day who were crying out to God for a sign . . . I wasn't crying that out at all. I already believed in God. I had

12. New King James Version, 2 *Corinthians 5:7*, www.bible.com
13. New King James Version, 1 *Corinthians 1:18–25*, www.bible.com

already been baptized and was repentant of my sin. I had already priori-tized him as the Lord of my life already and had said God, I will trust and obey you . . . even if you don't give me a sign . . . but please guide me Lord. I said in my thoughts/actions at the time, God, here I am, metaphorically, guide me. Though I did not use the actual words guide that night reading the bible . . . my heart however, was seeking him and seeking to please him and only him. The fact that God chose to give me a vindicated literal sign in the writing on the wall as a result of that test . . . was on him. He delighted in it . . . for his purposes alone. I didn't need it in order to be "saved" from God's wrath at my sin. I was already saved from that. But for the purposes of my journey after, I have of course clung to this event as a sign of proof of him and proof that I yet remain within his grace and favor, even with all the sinful twists and turns my life would take at times as my flawed theology was renewed and "fixed".

I suggest if you are demanding that God give you a miraculous sign before you believe in him and put your trust in him . . . that no sign will ever be good enough for you and your argument is inherently flawed and in God you will never place your trust.

That's all I'm writing for tonight. Though I know I will re-edit/add details above as part of the writing process.

Tomorrow, God-willing, I will write about the house, the next day, my reactions to the writing on the wall and what I did next. But in this story in this chapter . . . you have the gist of the most amazing event to have hap-pened to me yet. Though yet more context remains . . . and more strange events shall unfold. Including my incredible journey away from God/church for a time, before/after this event and my even more grace filled journey back towards God/church after this.

How could anyone fall away, even temporarily from their faith in God's church after experiencing the writing on the wall? Well, I did. And I thank God for his grace and guidance in being patient and long suffering with my strange reactions and stumbling blocks. It wasn't easy to be fully submissive and learn discernment and ultimately, I believe wisdom, which I also intend to share as a result of these amazing experiences.

I hope I have earned your attention enough now however, for you too, to keep reading.

Next: Chapter Two: At the House with the Writing on the Wall, The Next Day, My reaction . . . and the Greater Problem.

Chapter 2

Returning the Apple to the Tree or Out of the Land of Canaan into the Land of Haran

"'You will not certainly die,' the serpent said to the woman. "For God knows that when you eat from it your eyes will be opened, and you will be like God, knowing good and evil."'[1] — Genesis 3:4–5

BEFORE RETURNING THE APPLE TO THE TREE

Now this morning, I felt from the urging of God inside me, to share about the night I returned the apple of the tree of knowledge, metaphorically, to the tree and the beginning of my mental health journey, before continuing on the story of the writing on the wall.

Put simply, I went on another journey, this time on January 17, 2005 — a journey where I felt God was telling me to cease my judgmentalism as a christian and stop imagining that I was a better christian than I actually was.

You see, the next day, I was first diagnosed with Bipolar Affective Disorder by a psychiatrist.

Firstly, some context.

I had been attending Gateway Baptist at Mackenzie, Brisbane and found my passion for the Lord, in worship and example to my fellow Christian friends I'd made there or encouraged to attend with me.

---

1. New International Version, *Genesis 3:4–5*, www.bible.com

I became quite an outgoing chap (where once I had been very introverted) and people seemed to enjoy my company.

A few months earlier, 75 of my closest friends from the church and my family too, came to a hall I hired to celebrate my 30th Birthday.

Everybody was having fun.

Including me.

However, for some reason, as I look back on the events at this time and the night of the 17th of January 2005 in question, I can't help but equate this experience with the beginning of the book of Job . . . God beaming with pride . . . and Satan saying, that I was only such a good christian because God had sheltered me from how sinful I really was and so, by grace, had blessed my efforts . . . Maybe, I theorize, Satan argued that if God withdrew his guidance, grace and blessing, I would fall irrevocably away . . .[2] So God may have authorized a spiritual test . . . that it's playing out is part of the heart of this overall story I'm telling here.

During the first half of 2004, I had also been working as a counselor/social worker at a homeless youth shelter, before my refusal to bend the rules where a resident was bullying another resident was concerned meant I evicted the bully from the shelter in the middle of the night and lost my job after this was investigated by the management when the bully complained to them about being evicted. I felt hard done by, misunderstood, that I had behaved appropriately . . . but I simply moved on/back to high school teaching.

I then worked as a Secondary School Drama teacher for the next half of the year. I was the sole Drama teacher there, responsible for the entire curriculum, teaching 7 classes. In addition, I put on/produced/directed, several students in plays and their annual school musical as well.

I was also doing several dance lessons a week, as well as attending church and a bible study for young adults. (I was 29 at that stage.) As well as socializing with friends every spare minute I had.

I was definitely burning the candle at both ends. Draining the reserves of my seemingly endless energy and enthusiasm for God.

Near the end of the school year, I felt deflated . . . burnt out . . . and one morning, I just couldn't get out of bed . . . surprisingly . . . this resulted in some thought/introspection, so I resigned as a teacher.

After a couple of months of living on savings, I decided to get a job as a door to door mobile phone salesman. That brings us to January, 2005.

2. New International Version, *Job 1:6–12*, www.bible.com

In selling phones, I did really well, fantastically well . . . I sold phones to nineteen out of the last twenty-three places I went . . . This was unheard of . . . such a fantastic sales versus impression rate! However, my mind, had started to become unhinged . . . my thoughts were racing, I was speaking so fast, with so much enthusiasm . . . I made a mistake at work in going into a store that sold the phones, in seeking an answer to a question . . . and whilst there, I talked a customer into signing up with me (a better deal than the one in the store), rather than with the retail salesman. The retail worker complained to management and I was fired from the position.

But I was determined that there were no setbacks, only opportunities.

THE JOURNEY OF RETURNING THE APPLE TO THE TREE

So that night, I went and stayed at my elder sister's place (I also have a younger and an older brother), confiding to my sister that I had my energy back and I was ready for the next steps.

So, I opened my brother in law's bible that night, and suddenly, as I read, I had this sense from God . . . a lightbulb moment of realization . . . that all my life had led to this point . . . that meant, all my many sins in the past . . . had merely led me to the point of sanctification now . . . as a fully sanctified person . . . that meant I could now, possibly, be Jesus himself, filled with the spirit, in a new body . . . a body that I reasoned couldn't be killed again . . . for it had been raised imperishable . . . and the only way to put that to the test would be to put my life on the line and see what happened.

Flawed reasoning I know . . . brought on, by a season of overwork, stress, with poor boundaries . . . and whilst I had made time for God . . . in my naive eagerness to please him, I had allowed strange thoughts and reasoning to take over my mind.

Anyway, what happened next is a testament of God's grace (Grace when I use the word; I define it as receiving 'the unmerited favor of God'), as much as the beginning of a small miraculous journey . . . and my mental health journey and my journey away from God's church . . . even though in my heart at that point, all I was doing was seeking God, once again.

On a related side note; a facebook friend recently posted a quote I fully agree with; especially in matters of the Holy Spirit if I think I'm going to meet resistance from those close to me.

I quote her post now:

> Don't tell people what you're doing. Because if you do, and you're
> still implementing the very thing you said you would do, those
> people will look for all the reasons why it's not working, and why
> you're failing at it. "See! I told you so!" "See I knew it wouldn't
> work!" "See it was never going to work!" You don't need that. Hold
> firm and stand strong in your convictions . . . . . . You are just in
> the process of integrating things that others do not understand.
> When people don't understand, it's because they are coming from
> a limited perspective and positionality (sic) that they would rather
> hold firm to, than to consider the possibility of a new way. It's not
> your job to change their thinking. But it is your job to hold firm
> to your dreams. So friends, if you can help it (and I know that in
> many cases you can't . . .) don't tell them what you are doing.[3]

My attitude has ever been thus when those near and dear to me think
they know better than me who might wish to stand in the way of my tests
between me and the Holy Spirit in matters of conscience. If I think the
Holy Spirit wants me to do something and if I think telling a certain person
who might try to stop me will interfere with that; then I will simply follow
the Holy Spirit's promptings and let them find out after the fact. I must
answer to God[4] — first and foremost for my choices! Not friends or family.
Though of course, I know being on the receiving end of such a cavalier
attitude in my actions is not easy for any of those to handle at times either.
People understandably feel hurt and rejected about not being consulted or
included in the decision making process prior to me simply acting. If and
when I need differing opinions on the validity of my potential, current or
previous actions; I do however ask for them from whom I want them from.

So, I left my sister's house in the middle of the night, like I would
do years later in heading to Christchurch; not telling anyone where I was
going . . . I was determined to put myself on the line and conduct another
scientific test this time with the Holy Spirit, and see if God wanted to kill
me . . . and I was wrong about not being killable . . . or that God would have
grace on me . . . and I would pass the test and so he would keep me alive.

Now this story, I relate, in a certain way at the time . . . to Abraham's
test with Isaac. God had asked Abraham to sacrifice his son, to test his
loyalty . . . and in that story, just as Abraham was about to plunge the knife

---

3. Wimpenny, *Facebook News Feed Screenshot Friday 12th January 2024*
4. New International Version, *Romans 14:12*, www.bible.com

in, God provided a nearby sacrifice and Abraham was off the hook, having proved that there was nothing he valued more than God . . . having reasoned that God could do anything . . . even raise Isaac from the dead if need be.[5]

So did I value my life . . . more than I valued my love for God? I certainly did not.

So, I lay on the darkest stretch of road far from the streetlights, just under the rise of a hilltop, where I knew several trucks passed by regularly in the middle of the night full of groceries, with a large suburban grocery warehouse nearby.

And as I lay on the road, I shut my eyes and I said to God in my heart . . . "Lord I obey you first and foremost in all things. If you choose to sacrifice me now, so be it, into your hands I commit my spirit."[6] (Knowing at the time my thoughts were deliberately echoing Jesus' words on the cross.)

Then I heard the roar of the truck pass over me and I looked up and saw the truck in the distance.

I then felt that God asked me to do it again. So I found an even darker stretch of hill and lay sideways on the road . . . again, I told the Lord I committed my spirit to him . . . and again I heard the truck roar over me . . .

I then felt like God had proved his point to me . . . but then I felt an urging in my spirit to go on a journey rather than return the mile or so to my sister's house in a nearby housing estate. Now that I had proved to him and myself that I valued nothing more than God and pleasing him; God now wanted me to learn something else . . . but I didn't know what.

I started following a creek bed, which soon joined up with other waters and a mile or so later I was swimming in the water . . . still I continued to move downstream.

My clothes got heavy and I felt God tell me to ditch them . . . so I did.

Eventually, I reached a place where there was a large tree with branches hanging down over the water.

I felt God tell me to climb to the top of the tree . . . so I did . . . and as I climbed near the top, I felt God tell me to stretch out my hand, as if I had an apple in it and return it to the top of the tree . . . I was metaphorically returning the apple of the judgement of good and evil to the tree, refusing to eat of it, and merely trusting the Lord, that whatever he brought my way from here on . . . was his to give or take away . . . and I would cease labelling

5. New International Version, *Genesis 22:1–19*, www.bible.com
6. New International Version, *Luke 23:46*, www.bible.com

such actions as right or wrong and myself or others as doing the right thing or the wrong thing . . . and I would be blessed if I managed to put this into practice from here on.

Anyway, the branch I was sitting on, broke as soon as my hand with the imaginary apple in it touched the uppermost branch and I fell some five meters or so to the running creek water below.

Then I felt God tell me to leave the creek and get warm. I had learned the lesson he wanted me to know about judgement. The sun also had started to rise by this point.

I crossed a fence gap and found myself in a small housing estate. I knocked on a door, covered my nakedness with my hands, and the old lady who answered told me to go to the medical centre nearby. It seemed I was in a retirement village.

AT MENTAL HOSPITAL: THE RESULT OF RETURNING THE APPLE TO THE TREE

Inside the medical centre, the overnight nurse there let me in and called an ambulance.

I was taken to a local hospital and assessed by a psychiatrist as having Bipolar Affective Disorder (Mania with Psychosis) and admitted into their open ward for treatment and future discussion of my presenting issues with them.

That night, I felt God telling me to put him to the life test for a third time. So I pressed a fire alarm, jumped two fences and leapt directly in front of the first oncoming car. As I was struck by it, I felt as if invisible hands grabbed me and I was thrown over the car and I came to my feet as the car then stopped nearby.

I then lay down on the road, as if stunned. An ambulance nearby, picked me up and deposited me at the hospital's closed/secure ward this time, for further discussion and treatment.

During my stay there, I knew I had acted erratically, with flawed logic. They put me on mental health drugs, told me I had behaved strangely, and was lucky to be alive.

I was willing to accept that yes, the chemicals in my brain had gone strange, and I needed to "return to earth", and get some logic back in my brain. I was not in heaven and I was not some chosen vessel or messenger.

However, one thing remained with me throughout all this . . . and that was I knew God wanted me to cease judging mine or other's actions. Somehow, whatever the appearance of things . . . the real truth might always be different. Therefore I had no right to judge others or myself. (The need to still discern Good/Evil and the consequences of my/others actions that remain on my path of wisdom/sanctification are dealt with later in this story.)

What might look like a deranged suicide attempt . . . was actually an honest attempt of putting my life deliberately into the fullness of God's hands and holding nothing back from him in my value system. No love for friends, family, possessions, job or anything mattered at all to me next to God. Pleasing him was all that mattered.

Hosea 9:7 says " . . . The prophet is a fool, The spiritual man is insane . . ."[7]

This entire "dilemma" so to speak when such a scenario as detailed here occurs (and it doesn't always — sometimes man's wisdom and God's wisdom easily match) of the wisdom of men is foolishness to God[8] and wisdom of God is foolishness to men[9]; forms part of the underlying subplot of this entire novel.

In obeying what I saw as coming from God's Holy Spirit . . . I was acting erratically to outside observers who knew little of what was truly going on — though they thought they knew a lot. I valued pleasing God above man of course. "Man's wisdom" — says I was insane. But the spiritual man was only seen as insane by "man" because of man's inability to discern God's Holy Spirit at work as well in my example here of my inability to communicate that fact well previously. (Until the writing of what you are reading now at any rate.)

Indeed, my attempt to communicate "my side" of the story in this book; will hopefully leave the spirit-filled searcher in awe, amazement and wonder and praise God for what his Holy Spirit did with me. I hope that inspires you to hopefully take another step to value pleasing God/the Holy Spirit above man's opinions in your own spiritual walk that little bit more than you did before you came across my story and read my words here.

As for those who are closed in their spirit, to the Holy Spirit's presence and his attempt to communicate with them; doubtless what I've said here merely backs up their view already that I was insane, and that if indeed a

---

7. New King James Version, *Hosea 9:7*, www.bible.com

8. New International Version, *1 Corinthians 1:25*, www.bible.com

9. New International Version, *1 Corinthians 3:19*, www.bible.com

'spiritual man' is insane; then they want no part of such insanity. I hope that is not the impression my detailed testimony, journey, subsequent analysis, opinions and conclusions leave you with.

A DANGEROUS BOOK: FULL COMMITMENT TO THE HOLY SPIRIT COUPLED WITH NON-JUDGMENTALISM

For make no mistake — what I'm writing here is a "dangerous" book! I suspect some legalistic theologians, many psychiatrists and mental health professionals will declare this book "idiocy" and want it "burnt" for a potentially damaging influence on those with "delicate mental health." I am throwing down the gauntlet of a challenge to both Christians and Non-Christians who may read this book. Especially to those who are quick to judge and put me in a box of insane; psychiatrists, family members, even close friends who don't understand. It is "easy" to label me as "insane" — but the proof is in the results. And it is from the undeniable results that I am drawing my conclusions.

Regardless of what it felt like to be touched by the Holy Spirit; whether or not you think I was . . . (Does not the writing on the wall prove to you that I have been touched and that I have even dared to fully submit/allow the Holy Spirit to touch me?), during that three week stay, I came back to my "self", Justin Brent Wallace . . . realized how God had tested me and my values . . . and moved back home a few months later, still surrounded by a few loving friends and close family.

I also made a decision to hang around less people . . . so that 75 people in size group of close friends from Gateway . . . most of them went by the wayside. Including Tim regrettably, the once close friend who I've dedicated this story to.

Not because I didn't care for them anymore, but because I felt God wanted me to come to terms with what had happened and that I needed to make some practical improvements to my life and attitudes.

Part of which meant, that I felt God wanted me to move away from the church for a while. I had always been attending church and had had, a real passion and fire in my worship of him . . . but for all that discovery at church; I now felt, God wanted me to discover him in the real world and to stop judging him as not being present in the real world.

So, I began listening, for instance, to non-christian songs, seriously, for the first time . . . having previously had an almost exclusive diet of worship and contemporary christian gospel music.

There are many other instances of me doing this in all areas of my life, for the reasons I stated above . . . and a couple of other short mental health stays in hospital wards also took place between the night I returned the apple to the tree in January 2005 and found the writing on the wall in March 2007.

I did find that being in mental hospital was a very safe place emotionally, where I could vent what was really taking place in my heart and mind and my life . . . And though I knew the doctors, the nurses and fellow patients, some who became friends; wouldn't really fully understand . . . they each listened and they cared.

And slowly, but surely, I began to come to grips with this strange new non-judgmental existence I now found myself living.

I told you I left the church after all . . . but I didn't leave in rebellion to God . . . I left in seeking God . . . and this too, I think is important in helping explain my "falling away" . . . as I didn't truly fall away from my faith in God either . . . it was just that I no longer had a great moral compass and yes I sinned . . . even if I didn't think it was sin at times . . . My moral compass was skewed . . . and God had many important lessons to teach me on this journey, some of which I hope to share later in this story.

And so, having shared this essential, first step on the journey towards the writing on the wall, I am now ready to return to that house and return to March 2007, share what happened there, my reactions and the problems I encountered in moving on from that moment.

Chapter 3

At the House with the Writing on the Wall, the Next Day, My Reaction and the Greater Problem.

"But the one who does not know and does things deserving punishment will be beaten with few blows. From everyone who has been given much, much will be demanded; and from the one who has been entrusted with much, much more will be asked."[1] — Luke 12:48

THE PAINTER

. . . *"We the owners have gone away and if you read this you have our permission to stay as long as you like"* . . .

When I walked around the driveway to the back of the house and gently tried the rear door of the house for the first time and surprisingly found it unlocked, I gently closed it, and stepped back onto the small raised verandah there.

I was surprised in my scientific mind . . . but that too, could have been a coincidence. Maybe I just happened to choose the one house in the neighborhood, after having a conversation with God . . . where he told me it would be unlocked . . . that was unlocked . . .

I stepped back, still slightly uncomfortable about the challenge of entering the humble abode without permission.

---

1. New International Version, *Luke 12:48*, www.bible.com

Then, my eyes fell and focused on what looked like large writing on the rear wall. I read it in shocked disbelief.

Suddenly, I knew I had God's permission to enter this abode. A brief feeling of utter humility overwhelmed me, where I felt unworthy of having received such direction and grace from the Holy Spirit. Nevertheless, after a few moments, I entered the house, with wonder on my face . . .

Inside, I found a house devoid of most furniture, though there was an old couch in the living room facing the street. It was dark, but the house was illuminated by open louvers in the windows. There were no curtains and I could see the street out the front as a car drove past.

I then returned through the back door and sat on the verandah, just looking in wonder at the writing on the wall.

All their life, most people are after a sign of unarguable communication with God. And if they just had it, they would believe, and act accordingly. They would make him the Lord of their life, in every way, and dedicate every moment to spreading the good news that God undoubtedly exists, and what he says in the Scriptures is true.

And now, I had just been given that moment.

I had had a 30 second conversation with God in my mind, where he promised me a safe space to sleep for the night, where with the owner's full permission, I could break and enter. The back door had been unlocked. (So no breaking actually — that record technically remains intact to this day — Lol) The house was deserted. And the owners of the residence, had made it abundantly clear that if any traveler by faith had found that writing on the rear wall of their house . . . that he/she had their full trust and permission to stay there.

Talk about receiving an unlikely prophecy . . . immediately followed by its direct, equally unlikely, instantaneous fulfillment!

Furthermore; all my aimless steps and wandering . . . over 48 hours . . . all the strange encounters and situations I had faced on that journey . . . had led me to stand in front of this strange house . . . to choose the one place where a man or woman in faith had written in paint those words on the rear wall of the house . . . never knowing if anyone would actually read them and then gone away, never knowing for sure . . . why the Holy Spirit had urged him/her to paint that.

I would love to meet that person. I do not suggest that it was the literal hand of God who painted those words and they were for my eyes only. (I certainly did not see a hand appear and paint those words directly — a la the writing on the wall event from the book of Daniel.[2])

They certainly weren't an illusion as an event, some 9 hours or so later would prove for sure. Which I am getting to. The strange encounters aren't over yet!

But all in good time.

For now, I sat in wonder and marveled at God's majesty in guiding me across a proverbial 40,000 aimless steps . . . to being exactly where he wanted me to be. To teach me. To guide me. Yes. But also I believe to teach you. And guide you. Unseen reader though you may be to me.

Just as I was an unseen traveller to the owners of that anonymous residence in the suburbs of Christchurch, New Zealand.

After a short time on the balcony, I looked in the backyard, and there was an external, detached garage.

I tried the side door of the garage and walked inside, leaving the door open for light.

And this observation would prove important . . . There was a car inside and there were a number of boxes and furniture items.

Only the house was relatively deserted . . . here was the furniture.

I felt like I should leave the furniture alone. The owner had given me permission to stay in the residence; not to take any of the items in the garage.

After a few moments, I left the garage, closed the door and returned to the inside of the house.

After a moment of exploring, I found inside a small doorway, a ladder leading to a trapdoor. When I climbed the short ladder and opened the trap door, I found what looked to be an attic.

For some reason, it felt right to me, to sleep there. Kind of like an upper room.[3] I liked its symbolism, being familiar with the Bible.

So, I returned to where I had left my backpack, picked it up, and closed the attic door behind me and then closed the trap door. Took my sneakers off (I still had socks on). Used the small backpack as my pillow and promptly fell asleep. I was tired after all.

2. New International Version, *Daniel 5:1–30*, www.bible.com
3. New King James Version, *Mark 14:15*, www.bible.com

TEAM ANGEL

The next thing I heard, hours later, were voices below me, coming from the rest of the house.

Unlikely as it seemed, given the owners had gone away . . . it seemed the house had another couple of visitors.

I thought they might leave me alone. I lay there for a few moments, thinking about what to do.

There was bright light coming through the cracks between the planks of the roof I was sleeping near. I knew I had been asleep for some time.

Then I heard the attic door open, and someone climbing the short ladder and opening the trapdoor.

"Who are you?" a nondescript, aged in his thirties, white caucasian man in a business suit brusquely asked, upon seeing me rise slightly to look at him from where I had been lying on my side.

"I am no one," I replied.

"Well, no one. You had better leave. This house has just been rented today and the new tenants will be here in half an hour."

I looked at him blankly for a moment. The garage was full of furniture and a car! Something strange was going on here. What was this business of this house just being rented to a new tenant who would be moving in in half an hour? Something wasn't right.

"If you don't leave," the man replied during my moment of silence as I weighed up my response, "I will call the police."

I didn't want that or any further trouble with the authorities, having a mental health history . . . I might spend the next three weeks in a hospital in Christchurch . . . Oh the irony!

"What about the writing on the rear wall of the house?" I finally asked, finding my voice.

"How do you know about that?" the man responded quickly.

"You wouldn't believe me if I told you," I replied; not sure that this was the time and place to reveal all the details of the journey I was on. "Anyway, I've read it and it says I have the owners full permission to stay here as long as I like."

"Regardless, I want you gone as soon as possible, or I will call the police."

"All right. I'll leave. No need to call the police. Give me a few moments."

" . . . We'll be waiting downstairs to see you out."

The man stepped back down the builtin ladder and returned to his friend, where I could hear them speaking to each other, but not what they were saying.

(Crazy[4] by Gnarls Barkley just came on my iPhone shuffle mix (I have over ten thousand songs on my iPhone through iTunes. Mostly christian. But a couple of thousand of reasonably popular somewhat vetted, secular ones too.)

Ironic perhaps . . . I like to share irony and I have nothing if not a sense of humor surrounding all the events of my life. I like to entertain and be entertained.

Anyway, I grabbed my sneakers, trench coat, bag, and returned to the lounge room to put my sneakers on.

The man who had spoken to me was now on his mobile phone, talking to someone else. I picked up a few snatches of his conversation as I put my sneakers on and tied my shoes.

"No, he's leaving now," was what I heard.

The other one, who also looked like a real estate agent, judging by his well dressed, but unbranded business suit, watched me quietly. He seemed a few years younger than the man on the phone. But equally nondescript caucasian.

"God led me here," I told him.

"Uh huh," he replied dismissively.

I then, walked out the open front door, down the outside stairs, the house was low set, but seemed to be built up from the ground on stilts or something like that. I didn't pause too hard to investigate, I was keen to leave. Not wanting trouble with the Police and all that jazz.

Sometimes in the years since, I've wondered what the Police's reaction might've been to discovering me there; had I stayed and pointed out the writing on the rear wall of the house giving me permission. Would they have marveled about my reason for finding it at the journey I'd been on? What might've happened next? But anyway, it didn't happen, I moved on.

As I left the residence, I saw I was two houses from the corner, where there was some corner shop of some sort, now open for business. And then I turned the corner, and that was the last I ever saw of the house with the writing on the wall. Though I did return once 8 years or so later, on a holiday with a friend to Christchurch, partly in the hopes of finding that residence again. I did not.

4. Barkley, *Crazy*

Refreshed and less weary than the night before, as I walked, once again aimless miles through the suburbs of Christchurch, one of the largest cities in NZ, I mused about this strange event to myself. Then, and now, still. Attempting to make sense of it, and everything else happening too.

Were they really real estate agents, despite the inconsistencies in their story of a new tenant arriving soon? If so, why was there furniture, and a car, and boxes in the garage? Not to mention an old couch in the lounge room? Surely the new tenant if so, had moved some stuff in already. Including a car.

And if so, why would real estate agents show up, if the keys had already been handed to the new tenant; who had moved it seemed under such a scenario, some stuff in already? Surely, it would be the new tenant him/herself who discovered me in the upper room . . . and would demand that I move on, immediately . . . despite the writing on the wall.

But that wasn't what had happened. I can only present facts . . . and muse about their meaning.

Of course, the other scenario, was something that appealed to me as an answer too . . . but I could never know for sure whether it was true.

Had I just had an encounter with angels or even demons . . . Had I stumbled on some great secret place where people of faith would stay . . . and where they would be led and guided by angels or even demons . . . as part of some weird cosmic trial or testing of their faith? Or mine, in this instance.

I like to think . . . I had been entertained in a direct encounter by angels . . . with me, mostly, unaware . . . who weren't given permission to reveal themselves as angels . . . only to move me on from the residence with the writing on the wall where at one point as I fell asleep, I had thought about staying several days at least and using it as a base to explore Christchurch . . . But I don't know they were angels for sure . . . Either way, I felt unworthy of being touched by God as I felt I had been . . . and thought that was why he had wanted to remove me from my "identity" as Justin Brent Wallace before he led me to the writing on the wall. I also felt in a way as Peter did in the Bible at one point upon witnessing one of Jesus' miracles . . . Get away from me Lord, I am a sinful man . . . [5] I do not deserve knowledge of you or for you to have revealed yourself to me as you have chosen to do so.

What do you think? Which team are you on? Angels or Real Estate Agents? I'm curious to ask you that at this point. And if you ever have a way

5. New International Version, *Luke 5:8*, www.bible.com

of directly contacting me and discussing these events . . . I'd be very curious to hear your answer and discuss the scenario. Yet again.

Lord knows I've tried to make sense of this. But some things are maddening. (And I'm thinking of Dumbledore's moment where he uses that phrase to Harry in the movie Harry Potter and the Goblet of Fire . . . "Every time I try to make sense of why these things are happening Harry . . . it slips away . . . its maddening."[6]) God reveals what he wants, when he wants, for his reasons alone.

But either way, I had been given direct proof that it was the Holy Spirit that had led me through my wilderness to the writing on the wall. Giving me a direct prophecy and fulfilling it immediately, in a spectacular way. I knew the Holy Spirit was something that worked through God the Father outside me working in unison with his Holy Spirit inside me; guiding me, and if I was just prepared to listen, trust and obey him, I would be blessed and indeed, had just been blessed. (Even though it may be a slightly ridiculous moot point in "a spirit"; I've always thought of the Holy Spirit too as having a masculine identity, like the rest of the Holy Trinity . . . sorry ladies. ;)) The Holy Spirit in practice for me hence, is not easy to listen, trust or obey at all — especially when the instructions were so obviously foolishness in man's wisdom . . . though they did prove how God's marvelous wisdom was truly foolishness to man.

THE GREATER PROBLEM

So I now had greater knowledge of God, than the average church goer . . . through my experiences here . . . but I also had been given a greater problem of being asked to trust that inner voice of the Holy Spirit, far more, than the average church goer without such a verifiable experience would ever be asked to . . . To he whom much is given, much shall be asked of . . .[7]

But being prepared to listen; to put my faith in the voice of the Holy Spirit inside me and God by extension in order to learn how to trust and obey the Holy Spirit . . . and damn the consequences . . . why that takes a lot of faith and trust to do; even with the proof I'd found in the writing on the wall of the Holy Spirit living in me and guiding me. This demands constant discernment! So, learning and applying this in my life from then on, is also part of the greater problem, I now faced.

6. Newell, *Harry Potter and the Goblet of Fire*
7. New International Version, *Luke 12:48*, www.bible.com

For I had long had my own inner voice of self/sin . . . leading me . . . battling with the Holy Spirit inside me . . . Kind of like my own shoulder angel and demon (Thanks Kronk[8]) . . . But if I just listened to every inner thought I had that *might* be from the Holy Spirit without proper testing and acted on that, despite the morality issues concerned; e.g., breaking and entering . . . well, I really would be crazy.

Now that I knew for sure the Holy Spirit could speak in actual words in my head . . . along with other random thoughts, not from him but of my own design; I knew I would need to learn and exercise even greater discernment and wisdom than most would ever consider they might need. I needed to learn how to distinguish the Holy Spirit's voice from my own sinful thoughts and tendencies as well as discern this clearly apart from any other external emotional, personal, intellectual, or actual spiritual or physical demons that might try to influence me; now that I was someone in particular who was so open to hearing the voice of God/the Holy Spirit and completely committed to the Holy Trinity. This was because I was someone who knew *beyond all reasonable doubt* that God himself through his Holy Spirit had spoken to me in my head directly even as God the Father had so obviously prepared the way to the house in Christchurch ahead of my arrival.

Knowing this; I knew a greater measure of accountability would now be afforded to me by God . . . because I knew beyond doubt that the Holy Spirit was talking to me and that my subsequent actions would be even more under a microscope . . . As for you the reader, you *may* still have "reasonable doubt"; not having lived my story; a doubt that I understand from both the unbeliever and the believer who haven't lived my life and experienced what I've experienced . . . but this/your doubt my story here addresses directly. In many ways; that is the entire point of this book. Of me sharing everything I'm sharing here with you. I get it now. To prove the Holy Spirit is real and not an 'illusion'. And is like a voice in your mind . . . even a random thought at times . . . And I need to listen to the Holy Spirit in my life . . . regardless of where he leads me . . . and so too, do all the "called"[9] . . . for many ignore it. Call it nonsense. But . . . I also need to scientifically test it and discern that each thought I have that might be from him, is in fact from the Holy Spirit. As I put the scientific method of assessing that voice I heard in my head, to the test, by leaving Brisbane obediently, but still 'testing' and going

8. Dindal, *The Emperor's New Groove*
9. New International Version, *Matthew 22:14*, www.bible.com

to Christchurch to see what might await as the result. When I felt the call that night, I did question . . . was that my own diseased voice or was that his? But blessed be to God; it was his. He proved it to me. For his reasons! And I praise God and give him all the honor and glory for this!

" . . . for many are invited (called by the Holy Spirit in my inference here) but few are chosen."[10] (Who listen to completion in their faith[11] to the Holy Spirit in my inference here.)

I'll say it again... only the chosen dare to listen to the holy spirit to completion in their faith. To complete/work out their salvation with fear (to fear God more than man and value pleasing him more than man) and trembling.[12] For the Holy Spirit unarguably has been given to all[13] who believe in the trinity and what that obedience in practice represents. (All who are repentant of course — for even the demons believe . . . and tremble.[14]) I also think, though some might disagree, that all people have access to the Holy Spirit's voice inside them; regardless of whether they acknowledge themselves to be Christian.

In support of this idea; Joel 2:28 says ""And it shall come to pass afterward That I will pour out My Spirit on all flesh; Your sons and your daughters shall prophesy, Your old men shall dream dreams, Your young men shall see visions."[15] To me, that means we ALL have God's Holy Spirit poured out on us. ("Afterward" from the quote, in greater context in the passage, I interpret to mean as being after Jesus' first coming and before his second coming.) But I believe we do not all detect, listen, discern, submit to or obey the Holy Spirit in equal measure. Or when we do listen, we do this in a wide variance of quantity/quality in our respective lives.

This is not surprisingly at times for me a struggle of applying discernment and wisdom still today . . . But my journey has brought me some measure of insight, wisdom and control. Which I intend to reference here in the rest of this story.

Despite being chosen by God, for his purposes to go to Christchurch and being his vessel, I also refuse at this point and every point, to call myself a prophet in any way. Do not twist my words. I am merely someone who

10. New International Version, *Matthew 22:14*, www.bible.com

11. New International Version, *Philippians 2:12*, www.bible.com

12. New International Version, *Philippians 2:12*, www.bible.com

13. New King James Version, *Joel 2:28*, www.bible.com

14. New International Version, *James 2:19*, www.bible.com

15. New King James Version, *Joel 2:28*, www.bible.com

hears and heeds the Holy Spirit's voice *sometimes*; who attempts to set an example in this and who tries to encourage others to do the same.

As for prophecy, by old testament standards all it takes is for one prediction to be proven wrong and the verdict by law is to stone the false prophet.[16][17] I have made many false predictions. "I don't think it will rain tomorrow . . ." Bam! I was wrong! It rained!

I have however learned some control and been given I believe some guidance, experience and proof of the voice of the holy spirit speaking inside me and that is what I hope to share, hope you find inspiring and hopefully will encourage you to do more of in your own life's circumstances when the Holy Spirit is trying to reach you/guide you in some way.

For a time, since the apple on the tree moment, I was in the passionate, zealous category of simply not judging anything as sin, which I felt impelled to do from that night onwards and acted without a great moral compass for a number of years there in my zealousness to put my eager heart for God into action . . . So, after I put that apple proverbially of judging good and evil, back on the tree, I spent a number of years refusing to say anything was sin . . . Rape? Murder? Even God has his plan for that . . . (Not that I encourage or commit such major sins or anything truly illegal in our increasingly libertine culture, ever, myself) Whereas before returning the apple to the tree, I felt that most things were sin . . . and was a passionate, zealous, albeit judgmental christian. Which I liken to the apostle Paul's experience with Judaism . . . before Damascus.[18]

However . . . I now had this discernment learning problem . . . I was clearly being taught by the Holy Spirit . . . but I also felt the dangers in taking this trust too far . . . It was an easy misstep into doing something foolish like stepping in front of a truck again . . . (Which as you know I did twice and a car once referencing my own life-test in my previous chapter) and I'm aware Jesus said to the Devil; you should not put the Lord to the test (though I prefer the wording here in the NKJV translation 'tempt' — a slightly different connotation[19]) . . . and in my case, that is still true . . . unless you feel you have the Lord's permission to put him and his spirit to test whether the spirit speaking to you is God/the Holy Spirit or some other sinful spirit in a way . . . So utilize when necessary instead this passage in

16. New International Version, *Luke 20:6*, www.bible.com

17. New International Version, *Deuteronomy 13:5*, www.bible.com

18. New International Version, *Acts 7:58*, www.bible.com

19. New King James Version, *Luke 4:12*, www.bible.com

the Bible that asks us to test the spirits[20] — which I quoted in my introduction — which as I've explained even in the synopsis event summary that I clearly had the Holy Spirit's sovereign permission to put him to the test and try the back door of the house to see if he was right; that the house was unlocked, and deserted and that I somehow, amazingly, had the owner's permission to stay the night there.

Realizing I had permission from God to test the spirits constantly after the writing on the wall, as opposed to what might be labelled my foolish test when I returned the apple to the tree; which demanded God's grace or my death; I felt an even greater responsibility to learn/apply discernment, other than just for my own safety. Surely people would need to know of my journey and amazing discovery . . . as last time, I had kept to myself, and just a couple of people, the gist of my journey returning the apple to the tree; feeling it would be too difficult to get people to understand what I had been through. However, my miracle of the writing on the wall was definitely not for my eyes and ears alone. I knew I had a responsibility to act wisely and not do more foolish things — unless, such a particular request was also tested and scientifically proven to have come from God/the Holy Spirit of course.

"Go and tell of what the Lord has done for you . . ."[21]

I knew my miracle hadn't just been for my benefit alone.

After all, I fully trusted him already. If more proof was needed, none would be sufficient. Zeal for the Lord still consumed me in every waking moment. (And still does.)

Yes, I had discernment to learn . . . and the miracle would play it's part in that for me. It was both an important lesson as well as an important gift . . . but I knew others would need to be told what had happened . . . and not just what but why . . . I knew there was something bigger happening here.

And whether that bigger would just be a little sphere of influence of a few friends/acquaintances given a brief summary thus far over the years of this event in Christchurch . . . or whether the full details would be shared in a memoir focused on discerning the holy spirit like this, that might potentially reach hundreds and God-willing, thousands more . . . would be up to the Lord.

That too, is up to the Lord, even now as I type this. I have no traditional publishing contract (I do now just a few months later — Woohoo! Praise

---

20. New International Version, *1 John 4:1*, www.bible.com
21. New International Version, *Luke 8:39*, www.bible.com

God!) and I have to convince a reputable hopefully christian publisher to publish such a risky manifesto (Given my behavior and total commitment) on the Holy Spirit; that this work shows the miracles that take place when you trust him that as a theological book now and not just a memoir, also dares to encourage the readers to listen more boldly to their own inner voice, after reading this story I'm sharing.

Up till now to repeat; the summary now that you're familiar with the details . . . It has usually gone something like this with the hundred or so friends, and family members and even a few strangers, and atheists, I've told in person; all of whom react in wonder; but not quite sure what it then means for them:

SYNOPSIS OF THE WRITING ON THE WALL EVENT

My introduction usually goes something like:

"How do I know God exists?

I don't have faith in God anymore. I have knowledge of him. Like knowing the sun came up in the sky today because you can see it and feel it.

This happened because of my writing on the wall experience I had in Christchurch. Would you like to hear it? It'll just take a minute of your time to hear."

(Sure)

"One night in March 2007, I was reading the Bible and I felt a strong sense from the holy spirit to travel to Christchurch, New Zealand where I had never been before.

The next morning I flew there and after wandering around for a day and a half, I stopped in front of a suburban street like any other, and in a bit of righteous anger, I asked God why had he brought me here? What was the point?

Then I felt the holy spirit in my mind answer my righteous anger. "Because, you've trusted and obeyed me, I'm going to give you what you want most right now."

Immediately riches passed through my mind, before realizing that what I wanted most right now, was a safe place to sleep for the night. I was tired and weary.

"All right," the Holy Spirit said, "Turn down the driveway of this house you're nearest to, you'll find the back door unlocked, and you can sleep there for the night."

"Whoa," I replied, "I'm not comfortable breaking and entering. I've never done that before?"

"What if you had the owner's permission, would that make you comfortable?"

"I don't understand."

"I've put you to the test in coming this far . . . just put me to the test now. Try the backdoor of the house. It will be unlocked."

"All right Lord, I'll put you to the test."

And not only did I find the back door unlocked and the house empty but I also found painted in large red writing on the rear wall of the house "*We the owners have gone away and if you read this you have our permission to stay as long as you like.*"

He also fulfilled for me in the process, Psalms 139:4 "Before a word is on my tongue you, Lord, know it completely."[22]

And I finish often with this conclusion:

"So, getting the prophecy immediately fulfilled for me, put the final nail in the coffin. I had travelled over four thousand miles . . . walked aimlessly . . . to arrive at the one place on earth prepared in advance for my arrival. God exists. The Holy Spirit can put words directly into my mind. I know it. The odds of all that taking place with no God in existence are astronomical . . . same as the odds in my view of creation existing without a God . . . No God? Ha! Utter nonsense to me.

I know God exists. And I must live responsibly according to the knowledge I see before me as plain as day. I cannot live any other way and still be true to myself and what I know to be true."

Make of that what you will dear friend/non-christian/atheist/family member/stranger/christian etc.

But having said that summary . . . I then move on . . . they move on . . . and it also took me quite a while to summate my journey into a minute or so to say. It used to take 10 minutes and eyes would glaze over and the real point of proof of the Holy Spirit speaking as an actual thought like voice in words in my mind was completely lost as I got bogged down in the detail . . . Now the mere summary takes me roughly a minute to say with excitement and emotion/tears to as many people I meet in person as I get the opportunity to tell (Not everyone sadly). Yes it means that much to me to share to everyone I can. Even now.

22. New International Version, *Psalms 139:4*, www.bible.com

And this moving forward in my life, now that I had properly understood what was taking place and learnt some greater discernment of good and evil . . . would take some time to master. Including learning to contain my naive eagerness to simply obey every urge I thought *might* be from God. Not to mention contain my occasional rebellion against holy urges and being sinful and listening to the sinner inside me . . . so moving forward/ greater sanctification would take me some time to fully master.

And in my own journey of sanctification . . . I can tell you the closer you get to God . . . the more clearly you can see your own sin and your own struggles . . . and know just how far short of God's glory you are . . . [23] So I am still nowhere near as discerning or sanctified as I would like to be . . . I still fail and fall . . . far too often for comfort. Even in areas where I never thought I would fall or had a problem with at all. But I still repent too. Fall on my knees before God and beg him not to lose patience with me. I refuse to let sin win and get in the way of my relationship with God. And that really, is the most important thing in life to learn.

THE MOTEL

So this leads me back to Christchurch now . . . and why, I decided to spend my remaining money on a nameless motel I reached late in the afternoon there, for the night . . . to allow what I was seeing on the TV in the motel, to influence me and see if there were any messages directly for me in it. And if so, what they were . . .

And those messages were all about a great spiritual battle taking place unbeknown by most . . . for not just my soul, but your soul and every other soul that exists, will exist or has ever existed. All from watching the movie "National Treasure"[24]; starring Nicholas Cage and Sean Bean that night!

This was all way too much for my poor brain to cope with the next morning . . . so I knew I needed a safe place to consider everything and make sense of what was going on in my head, my life and others lives . . . so I concocted a plan to get myself arrested for loitering. As Hebrew 10:16 says "I will put my laws on their hearts and minds."[25] God's law was on my heart and uppermost in my mind. I also take note of what Peter and John said,

---

23. New International Version, *Romans 3:23*, www.bible.com

24. Turteltaub, *National Treasure*

25. New International Version, *Hebrews 10:16*, www.bible.com

when arrested in the Sanhedrin "we must obey God rather than man"[26] — so is loitering a sin when you are told by the Holy Spirit to loiter/get arrested? So while loitering may be illegal — there are contexts when illegal is not sin. I felt loitering would get me admitted to Christchurch Mental Hospital as soon as possible . . . where I felt I would be safe . . . to speak my thoughts . . . with both the patients and the doctors. Though I knew they would all write off my ramblings as crazy. I understood that all too well. But I also had a responsibility not to believe them that I was crazy. I knew what I had experienced in the writing on the wall. God had given me a great gift and what I would do with it, someday, was important, I knew that.

I had no more money anyway and I knew I had learned from God, in terms of a miraculous encounter with the Holy Spirit, what I had left Brisbane a few days ago now, to learn.

So I simply sat on a bench at the motel and refused to leave after checking out of my room. I stayed silent and unresponsive. Like Jesus did when he was face to face with accusations at times.

The police were soon called. I was arrested. I had no identification on me. No money. (The last $94 went to the motel owner in cash, where the room cost $99 for the night. He was a good sport and let me stay for $94.) I refused to speak to them. I was put in a holding cell at a watch house for the night. During the night, I decided to tell the guard I had a mental health history under the name of Justin Brent Wallace. I thought that might speed matters up. I was anxious for a proper bed in a mental ward and hungry for other food after 3 days of eating a half-chicken bought from red rooster at the Brisbane international airport before I flew to Christchurch.

The next day, I was brought before a judge who ruled a mental health assessment should be undertaken and I was transported to Christchurch Hospital and admitted for what became 3 weeks as a patient.

There, many strange encounters took place . . . (I don't wish to double the size of this book) it was all important for me however, to "come to my senses"[27] . . . to come back to myself . . . to try and understand this amazing journey I had been on and what God had revealed to me. I told some of it to the Doctors and my concerned Mother on the phone from Brisbane. She had been in Sydney visiting my younger sister until I disappeared and didn't come home for dinner, the evening after I left the house to travel to Christchurch. Yes, I lived with my parents; my mother and my stepfather

---

26. New International Version, *Acts 5:29*, www.bible.com
27. New International Version, *Luke 15:17*, www.bible.com

that night in Brisbane. I was unemployed at that point; because my contract as an administration officer simply hadn't been renewed a few weeks earlier with the Government; last hired/first let go etc. My stepfather wasn't in Sydney however. He alerted my mother to start a search for me.

After 3 weeks in Christchurch, I flew home at my mother's expense and attended an appointment with a treating local mental health clinician and allowed to go home. My answers were "sane" in their view, I was in no danger and no danger to others and I was heavily medicated on antipsychotic and mood stabilizers . . .

After a time, I picked myself up and started studying again. Still struggling to make sense of this writing on the wall experience; coupled with my journey of non-judgmentalism from the apple on the tree night, years before.

I knew I had been given some great gifts . . . but I didn't know what to do with them, nor how to truly communicate about them, without coming off as crazy . . .

So the next chapter will focus on my response to these events, and cover a number of years since. I have titled it "The Gospel According to Justin" and it is a changing gospel of maturing wisdom . . . as my understanding deepened and my attitudes warranted changing . . . but it is still a gospel of passionate faith in practice . . . albeit misplaced at times as I see . . . leading to the following chapter of sins/stumbling blocks . . . which I have labelled "Confession Time". Which I see as necessary to me to reveal in order to move forward and not have any reader get a better impression of me because of my faith experiences in any way. Give God the glory. Not me. I am truly not deserving of any . . . and I got myself in trouble many times . . . particularly with the ladies . . . I have had a hard time in being single too and not placed enough faith in God that he would bring the intimate godly relationship I desired with someone into my life . . . So much so, that on more than one occasion, I rebelled and took matters into my own hands — which only led to more sin . . .

I kind of liken that chapter to David's issues with Bathsheba[28] . . . capable of such great faith in confronting Goliath[29] and emerging victorious and vindicated . . . like I did in discovering the writing on the wall, albeit through a lot of faith in God being asked of me, by the Holy Spirit . . . but I'm also capable of utterly rebellious, seemingly faithless non-judgmental

28. New International Version, 2 Samuel 11, www.bible.com
29. New International Version, 1 Samuel 17, www.bible.com

acts . . . knowing God would forgive me . . . so I might as well use my "christian liberty" to sin . . .

Chapter 4

The Gospel According to Justin

"'Do not judge and you will not be judged.'"[1] — Matthew 7:1

LIVING NON-JUDGMENTALLY

I stopped attending a church regularly for the first time in February 2005, leaving Gateway Baptist in the aftermath of the returning the apple to the tree night and my first mental health diagnosis/hospital stay. At the age of 30.

I was still a christian of course and am determined to say that my faith in God and Jesus as my savior has never truly wavered; especially not since the writing on the wall in March 2007. I've always repented and believed in him, since I was six years old when my mother bought me a children's Bible which I read voraciously. Saying nightly prayers as a youngster and always being that kid in Sunday school, who knew all the answers to all my teachers' Bible story questions.

But in 2005, I felt I had been called to live a less judgmental life . . . and my own recent experiences had shown me that seemingly crazy actions could have pure motives . . . so I felt called in a way, to leave the church for a time in order to discover more of how God worked in the world.

Perhaps it was a mistake to do so; it certainly led me into sin at times . . . but it also led me to a deeper understanding of sin, grace, and morality and ultimately discernment, and wisdom than I had before.

---

1. New International Version, *Matthew 7:1*, www.bible.com

At that time, I still read my Bible, somewhat regularly, though daily devotions started to cease as being regular. I would read the Bible when I felt led to do so. And not do so, when I didn't feel led by the spirit to do so. That meant weeks passed at times, with me failing to read it . . . while at other times, I would spend several hours reading it. My regular pattern of 30 minutes of nightly reading before bedtime; a habit I had maintained for the best part of 25 years; was altered.

I also sold hundreds of my christian music Cds . . . as I was determined to listen more, in a discerning way, to non-christian music . . . to try and find God's messages in the lyrics . . . and the reasons why he had chosen to bless this music with popularity.

I believe God always has his reasons in allowing Satan the freedom he's had since the fall . . . even if Satan is referred to by Jesus as 'the prince of this world'.[2]

And, now that I was looking, I found God's messages in many pieces of music, events, movies and even general conversation with unbelievers . . . often hidden in a lateral interpretation; rather than the obvious literal . . . but still there nonetheless.

I had a brain that was switched on and capable of reading multiple interpretive messages from the same line of communication almost instantaneously/simultaneously; whether that was audible, read, or visual/shown in movies or on television or even advertising.

To see both the concrete and the abstract . . . though too much abstract thinking at times was leading my brain to overcook and I had a couple more hospital stays before the writing on the wall in Christchurch (which was my fourth short stay in a mental ward).

Rather than go into extreme detail about those other two presenting circumstances; I'll just summarize and make comments that are relevant regarding those. There was no great illumination/revelation from God/ proof of the Holy Spirit speaking to me, like with my first visit/apple on the tree; and with my deliberate fourth visit in Christchurch; immediately post the writing on the wall.

What happened; in general; was that my logic receptors were going astray and I was struggling to discern the Holy Spirit and the right way to behave appropriately from too much abstract thought . . .

2. New International Version, *John 14:30*, www.bible.com

On one occasion, I stripped down naked in my parent's house and loudly declared I had no shame . . . having lost touch with reality slightly . . . Naturally my concerned mother called an ambulance . . .

On another occasion, I walked head first into oncoming traffic . . . feeling that it would part for me, like with Moses' parting the red sea[3] . . . because I was special . . . and it did. But I wasn't special. I was losing touch with reality from too much heaven on my mind/abstract thought and those around me could see that . . . an ambulance was again called . . . and I was re-admitted a couple of times for a short time and dosed up again on mental health drugs, having dropped off the mental health drugs at times since being released back into the world, feeling I no longer needed them. (I did — and have actually been stable on the drugs since my last admission over 8 years ago now — the last admission, I will also get to later in this story.)

To repeat; my diagnosis was Bipolar Affective Disorder . . . meaning I had no problem with depression . . . just mania (containing my excitement/ joy) and losing touch with reality and being unable to discern appropriate ways of social interactive behavior with the right moral compass at times.

During this time, I started dating a fellow mental patient — a non-christian . . . and not wanting to judge my actions or hers as sin at that point; being determined to follow through on the lesson of non-judgmentalism from the apple on the tree night; I slept with her. Feeling somewhat justified that it wasn't sexual immorality . . . (It was of course; but my moral, intellectual and even spiritual receptors were all somewhat skewed at that point — and I had thrown the proverbial baby of discernment/morality out with the bathwater of "unjust" judgmentalism — as opposed to discerned "just" judgmentalism.[4]) Taking to a stupid extreme, Matthew 7:1.

That began a tenure of around ten years where I would almost exclusively date and "sleep with" non-christian women. Whereas before January 17, 2005; I had never gone out on a date or even considered becoming interested in a non-christian woman.

I did show interest in a couple of christian women after returning to my mother's church a couple of years after the writing on the wall; but rejection from them (essentially for not having my life set up and having it appear a little shambolic) led me to rebel and basically seek the arms of a woman who just wanted to care about me; even if she wasn't a christian. And at this time, it was easy for me to connect with non-christians because

3. New International Version, *Exodus 14:1–31*, www.bible.com
4. New International Version, *1 Corinthians 6:3*, www.bible.com

I was being so non-judgmental. Which is what those in rebellion to God most want of course — not to be judged for it. Just loved and accepted with all the flaws they refuse to deal with and maybe even enjoy.

As for "special messages" — a sure sign according to my psychiatrists of someone losing touch with reality . . . they've occurred for me ever since that night of January 17, 2005. A part of my brain lights up . . . I just heard for instance from my television (which was left on when I started to type this chapter) "Apparently, I have an apprentice." (One of the characters just said this to another character in the unknown midday Christmas movie which just happened to be on) . . . A special message makes me aware that this comment could be from the Holy Spirit directly to me . . . speaking in pride . . . "Apparently, I have an apprentice in Justin . . . who wants to know me, listen to me and hear and discern my voice . . . " A lateral, non-literal out of context meaning of that dialogue from the television . . .

I immediately switched the television off; partly to keep in control in my mind/focused on what I'm writing here . . . and resumed instead the background stimuli of my iPhone's extensive music collection . . .

That is just one example of this . . . There are literally thousands of other literal and lateral messages I've had from such non-christian or christian stimuli in the last eighteen years or so.

MOVING ON BEYOND THE WRITING ON THE WALL

Anyway, my gospel . . . was becoming confused . . . murky . . . it was difficult for me to discern . . . accurately . . . the course my life should take . . . and what God wanted me to do next . . . and so, move on beyond the writing on the wall.

Eventually, I decided to pick myself up after the writing on the wall, make a solid decision and in September 2007, I applied to go back to University to seek a career change. I felt my lateral brain would be good at marketing . . . so I studied a Masters in Marketing and also went back to attending a church regularly. My mother's local Baptist Church.

I did well at Marketing but towards the end of the first year of the two year course, I extravagantly asked a lady at my mother's church out . . . Perhaps I was losing my grip, in the manner of asking . . . even though, strangely enough I felt the Holy Spirit urge me to be overtly extravagant. The church pastors thought it was too extravagant and asked me to not

approach the lady in question again . . . detail, I may share at a later point
. . . the point now is to summarize; I felt embarrassed and moved forward.

So, given their reaction, and my own embarrassment, I felt called by
God to stop attending that church and the next Sunday night (when I'd
normally be at church), having checked my spam email folder on a whim
(not having checked it for months) where the audition notice email was, I
went to a community theatre audition and got the lead male part.

And so, began some extensive community theatre involvement, filmmaking journeys and screenwriting journeys still being a christian but not
attending a church for many years.

However, prior to my final hospital visit in December 2015, I started
reading the Bible again . . . and one verse in particular leapt out at me. It was
the solution to my discerning problem . . . my antidote to my twisted liberal
reality/morality of non-judgmental living . . .

It would send me back to church and ultimately help me come to my
senses.

MY ANTIDOTE TO NON-JUDGEMENTAL LIVING

That verse was First Corinthians 6:3 "Do you not know that we will judge
angels? How much more the things of this life!"[5]

(Another good verse which also convicted me in the last few years
since was Hebrews 5:14 "But solid food is for the mature, who by constant
use have trained themselves to distinguish good from evil."[6] — and indeed
for years I was immature and refusing to do this in practice because of my
twisting of Matt 7:1 into refusing to judge sin as sin)

I read that verse in First Corinthians late one night before bed in my
trusty 25 year old NIV study Bible on one of those rare whims to read the
Bible; and like a light bulb, I felt the holy spirit prescribe to me what my
biggest problem had been. And what I needed to do about it.

I needed to start discerning morality again. There was absolute good
and absolute evil. Not to condemn sinners myself . . . but to clearly see sin
. . . and what should be avoided in my or other's lives — to firstly "remove
the plank from my eye" in order to ever be able to help others with their
"specks"[7].

---

5. New International Version, *1 Corinthians 6:3*, www.bible.com

6. New International Version, *Hebrews 5:14*, www.bible.com

7. New International Version, *Matthew 7:5*, www.bible.com

In my naive exuberance to do this immediately following this realization however, I lost touch with a bit of reality in my excitable conversation with a friend and an ambulance was called and I was admitted to mental hospital for the 8th and final time as I type this.

But I was merely working my way through all my actions in the previous ten years since finding the Writing on the Wall. (From March 2007 to January 2016)

Anyway, once released from that stay in January 2016, I began picking myself up from the ground. I kept up screenwriting and acting but also went back to work as a bus driver . . . lost my job because of too many accidents (minor scrapes on kerbs).

Developed Irritable Bowel Syndrome hereafter called IBS (having gained weight on the mental health drugs); which meant I couldn't return to teaching either . . . not being able to hold my toilet.

Went back again to my mother's church . . . didn't feel accepted there as that lady was still there as I felt she was silently judging me . . . so I switched to another local Baptist church.

Got involved in a couple of Bible study groups and one church's video sermon filming ministry.

I had made a number of films in the previous ten years; including a feature film distributed on Amazon Prime worldwide as a streaming movie on demand. That was largely between 2010 and 2020 . . . indeed one of those mental health stays occurred (not the last one) when I lost sight of reality on signing the deal with the distributor — it went to my head — and I lost all concrete logic for a day or two there and became too lateral/abstract and was hospitalized.

And those films, had my own stamp of Justin's strange non-judgmental gospel attached to them . . . (Nonetheless the film was designed to ask the viewer serious theological questions and posit potential responses/answers from the viewers.)

That feature film's title was "Immortality"[8] (a 102 minute sci-fi movie drama) and it's premise was "A new drug is invented that ends aging in the human body, starting in the early twenty-first century and charting the course of the main character's life and how he and society adapts to no longer needing to live a fast paced life and make quick decisions with the 'end point' of death, no longer fast approaching; over the many centuries that follow." It was essentially a Christian's comment on what eternal life might

8. Wallace, *Immortality*

look like on earth and its existential challenges if the Atheists' assumptions were right and there really was no God.

Yes, I sole-produced it, directed it, edited it and wrote it. But over 200 people I involved in its 3 year production. Self-funded by God's grace through working pretty much full time hours/shift-work in security at the airport; with the film's planning taking place around my shifts, and taking holiday days for the shooting blocks. And I saw his hand everywhere in it and upon it; as most people who were skilled agreed to be involved for free.

Anyway, now that I had discovered First Corinthians 6:3; I had come back to God and my senses, truly.

LIVING A CORRECTED LIFE OF NON-JUDGMENTAL LIVING THAT EFFECTIVELY DISCERNS GOOD AND EVIL

But my life was still a bit messy and needed to be sorted out.

I needed a job I could do; and my IBS settled in the afternoons, so I got an afternoon job as a warehouse assistant. Hurt my back and changed to the job I now have, which doesn't use heavy lifting . . . in a kitchen at a hospital as a food service assistant delivering food trays to the hospital beds and doing dishes and suppers, whilst still doing creative writing like this/ filmmaking etc. It is a 'concrete' job that leaves me mentally fresh for my creative endeavors.

I also moved closer to my new job; and I changed to a more local church.

Gateway Baptist once again. Truly my life had come full circle. I even live in Greenslopes now where I lived last time, eighteen years before when I had the night where I put the apple of judgmentalism back on the tree.

And my plan now; in addition to promoting this book/my testimony of the Writing on the Wall I hope at any church or Bible study interested; is to get involved with some church drama productions. Gateway is a large community church and I hope opportunities will prove fruitful there to utilize some of my dramatic talents and possible filmmaking skills too. I also want to write a follow up book to this; as I know reading this story may encourage people to share their own stories of faith in God vindicated by proof with me; and I hope to gather their relevant details, and compile like the good journalist I was trained to be all those years ago, into an inspiring volume.

I have also written a number of christian plays, musicals, screenplays — one of my screenplays won a couple of years ago Best Unmade Screenplay and Fan Favorite at a U.S. International Christian Film Festival (as well as other stories aimed at guiding non-christians/seemingly non-christian stories).

I am hopeful for the future and hopeful that this story as presented here is appreciated by all those who encounter this and especially those who are seeking to better see and discern the holy spirit in their life and to apply his guidance and spiritual lessons to their lives.

However, my problems with discernment since the writing on the wall and the night of returning the apple to the tree in January 2005 might've been over . . . I now had the baby of discerned morality back, with just the bathwater thrown out of un-discerned immorality . . . but the greater problem of my sanctification . . . and moving beyond sinful tendencies now confronted me. Last year. 2023. Hence leading me to the next chapter.

Chapter 5

Confession Time and Discerning the Holy Spirit in My Life

"Therefore confess your sins to each other and pray for each other so that you may be healed. The prayer of a righteous person is powerful and effective."[1]
— James 5:16

MY STUMBLING BLOCKS

I have always held, fundamental reformed protestant conservative christian views. I have not been liberal or pentecostal or catholic. Despite studying and completing a graduate diploma in christian counseling through a pentecostal Bible college in 2003.

This means if the Bible called it sin. I called it sin. No grey area. Or leeway for me, till I returned the apple to the tree at least . . .

Then I went on the journey I told you about here.

But in discerning true morality from flawed morality/sin, I now had some catching up to do to reconcile fundamental moral views of behavior and years of bad non-judgmental habits and sinful practices.

Getting my heart and attitudes together would not be easy. I had a number of stumbling blocks to living well and it took me a while to discover each in turn and overcome them.

I still felt rebellious towards God and even harbored some resentment in being used as a pawn . . . for his schemes . . . He did lead me to the Writing on the Wall after all . . . and one of my reactions was to feel used . . . It

1. New International Version, *James 5:16*, www.bible.com

wasn't a good reaction of course. But at times, I'm ashamed to say I felt that way even though I knew he had given me greater proof of him and hence a greater blessing, than he gives to most.

Listening to the Holy Spirit to me really is like opening Pandora's Box . . . sometimes it seems strange . . . almost insane . . . often counter-intuitive . . . yet the Holy Spirit can be detected and discerned. "It" doesn't want to lead you to sin . . . it wants to refine you . . . to lead you closer to God . . . to becoming more Christ-like . . . more sanctified . . . in the end . . . than you were before.

Not less . . . and sometimes to become more sanctified . . . you have to become aware of your sin . . . it is often an unpleasant discovery. It is also unpleasant to discover just how much a part of you loves this sin . . . and clings to it . . . and doesn't want to let it go . . .

"Just let me be a sinner please . . . let me do the little things I enjoy doing . . . don't take away all the fun . . . Jesus your yoke doesn't seem real easy or light[2] . . . if I have to give up my secret sins . . . "

In my case, my secret sexual fantasies . . . for lust and pleasure . . . occasional self-gratifying and porn . . . my biggest stumbling block preventing me from being an effective servant for God.

I never had weaknesses for drugs or alcohol or gossip or lying (unless that is lying to one's self at any rate).

No, my weaknesses were tied into bad attitudes surrounding sex, women, and pleasure.

It was like a drug to me however . . . whenever I felt down, rejected, misunderstood, lonely . . . self-gratifying to porn would make me feel better . . . though I actually felt worse . . . mired deep in sin and unsure of how to pull myself out of this deep pit that I was in.

My most listened to song in my top 25 songs played list on my iTunes is "Too Many Times" by Michael W. Smith.[3] Still and has been for many years. It is a sad lament one feels about falling into sin. (And sadly there aren't enough laments in music in general these days I feel — though that leads to a discussion of other issues which I won't look at here.) Essentially the song message is too many times have I fallen into sin and asks the question in a yearning way; will I ever finally be the person you intend me to be God?[4]

2. New International Version, *Matthew 11:30*, www.bible.com

3. Smith, *Too Many Times*

4. Smith, *Too Many Times*

Great question . . . especially for someone like me struggling with my sin.

For years, I tried substitution . . . like a coca cola addict on caffeine, who starts to drink coffee because it isn't quite as bad for him as coca cola is . . .

Essentially, I was seeking a girlfriend . . . because I couldn't get my lusts under control . . . (See the apostle Paul's statements regarding unmarried virgins and widows burning with lust being better to marry and so have some semblance of control over those lusts.[5])

But the issue, whether or not I had a girl . . . was that I was full of lust and had a lack of self-control at times. I even felt rebellious anger towards God as what I saw as his failure to bring a godly christian woman into my life (who was interested in me and vice versa — I've met plenty who are godly who weren't into me).

And this year, the problems continued. Yes, there's repentance, guilt and shame but at times that hasn't been enough to prevent repeat offending and I've sunk deeper into the sin.

I just wish I had solved the problem . . . that I didn't have the weaknesses that I do.

At the moment, the problem is still there, though it seems somewhat under control . . . It is my "thorn in my flesh"[6]. And I fervently pray God helps me solve the issue.

As much as I wish I had've completely overcome this problem; I'm reminded of Second Corinthians 12:9: "But he said to me, "My grace is sufficient for you, for my power is made perfect in weakness." Therefore I will boast all the more gladly about my weaknesses, so that Christ's power may rest on me."[7]

I certainly don't boast in a proud way about my weaknesses . . . nor the fact that I still need God's grace in this . . . but in God . . . that he still loves me and can still help me despite my weaknesses. That because of his boundless grace, he hasn't given up on me. That in my weakness; that he even wants to make something beautiful of me. Even if the "how" he can do that remains a mystery when I look at the weak man that I am.

For now, I try to focus on him and what he would have me do with my life . . . and just kind of live with my weaknesses . . . like living with a

5. New International Version, *1 Corinthians 7:9*, www.bible.com
6. New International Version, *2 Corinthians 12:7*, www.bible.com
7. New International Version, *2 Corinthians 12:9*, www.bible.com

flatmate you don't particularly like, but have to put up with for the time being.

I hope these confessions will help you, the reader, understand, that for all the progress I've made with detecting and discerning the holy spirit's voice and finding my way back to my passion for the Lord and total dedication in my life to serving him; that I very much remain a work in progress, and better discerning of the Holy Spirit alone, and getting proof of that, won't simply remove sin from my life. No matter how much I might wish it did! I am full of flaws and even contradictions in a way.

The world has this impression of Christians who repent that they turn from their sin and it is so easy to never fall back into sinful habits . . . The reality of being a christian is you are constantly aware of your sin . . . It makes you appreciate God's grace and want to give him the praise for not giving up on you and that makes you even more repentant of it when you fall victim to those urges in yourself . . . and it remains a constant battle to defeat the sinner in you and listen to the Holy Spirit on an ongoing basis and emerge more sanctified than before.

Of course Christians are saved/justified by Jesus' propitiatory blood through faith and repentance restoring us in our relationship to God where he sees us as a white sheet . . . pure as Jesus who bore our just punishment so we don't experience God's final wrath and judgment. This is the justification part of the gospel which I've applied mostly as assumed knowledge in this book by the reader — my main focus is on my/yours sanctification/detecting the Holy Spirit — but for those readers who don't know; what makes Christ a suitable sacrifice to take God's wrath and punishment that I deserve? He lived a perfect life. Never sinned. Not even once. God's law requires perfection. And he was/is perfect. In taking God's just wrath for our sin on the cross . . . God exercised perfect justice and mercy with the one act.

However all actions have consequences. Jesus suffered the consequences of my sin. But Jesus was perfect and so God remains both perfect in justice and mercy. Once his wrath at our sin was satisfied, it was right, just and merciful for him to raise Jesus from the dead . . . giving him the gift he most wanted . . . and enabling those who repent of their sin who believe in him . . . to also share in Jesus' resurrection and hence, gain eternal life. So God's forgiveness was now possible — and our restoration of our perfection/relationship with God "justification" hence is through Jesus' efforts and not a result of our own efforts. "For it is by grace you have been saved, through faith — and this is not from yourselves, it is the gift of God — not by works, so that no one can boast."[8]

So, all I can do now is focus on the Lord, do my best to listen to the Holy Spirit and try to overcome my issues.

As I consider the near future, I hope and pray that God blesses my creative theological writing efforts such as this as well as keeps helping me overcome "the sin that so easily entangles"[9] me.

WISDOM LEARNED FOR HOW TO DISCERN THE HOLY SPIRIT'S VOICE IN MY LIFE

Repent of my sin, first and foremost. It clouds my mind.

Once repented, having listened to the Holy Spirit . . . it is not easy to always successfully detect and discern. So often my own voice interrupts . . . changing/altering the message . . . muddying the otherwise crystalline waters.

Will the Holy Spirit direct you to do some of the seemingly crazy direction/tests I was given?

Most unlikely.

I've tried to explain in my story here that for God's reasons, I was given the test that I was given . . . and the reward of having the Holy Spirit prove to me that he was speaking inside my mind, and it wasn't just my own imaginary thoughts, when I immediately found the writing on the wall, following that prophecy that I would have the owner's permission just before I found it. (Again, also proving/fulfilling Psalms 139:4 "Before a word is on my tongue, you, Lord, know it completely."[10])

Such nights/quests/internal direction from the Holy Spirit are rare in my life. The two main occasions this has been accompanied with a spiritual and literal journey, I've related here. Most of the time/rest of my life, like you, I just live my life and make decisions based upon the largely realistic parameters surrounding all my life decisions — but importantly, including asking the question . . . God, is this what you want me to do? Help me decide etc.

However, the impression of the holy spirit would have been ignored by me on those nights, had I not been an *avid* follower of Christ . . . *open,*

8. New International Version, *Ephesians 2:8–9*, www.bible.com

9. New International Version, *Hebrews 12:1*, www.bible.com

10. New International Version, *Psalms 139:4*, www.bible.com

trusting, submissive, and *obedient* to listening/hearing what the Holy Spirit was directing me to do, think or say and importantly, valuing pleasing him more than pleasing myself or 'man'. I was dedicated in my heart to doing what would please him, more than others or myself — if/when a call from the spirit means that I can't please God, myself and others all at once of course. The easier directions to follow from the Holy Spirit can often fit within that category; I add with a wry smile.

It is my fervent prayer, that as a child of God . . . that *if* you feel it *might* be the Holy Spirit directing you . . . feel free to scientifically put the spirit to the *test* in so doing as I did . . . (Is the piece of direction actually from the Holy Spirit or for instance, your own flight of fancy/diseased imaginings?) More than anything however, I'd encourage you to both listen and obey the Holy Spirit; even more so if you're sure the piece of advice may come from him. There is a reason for his directions. Even if you cannot see it immediately, and even if you don't get instant vindication for the test 48 hours later, like I did with the writing on the wall.

As the line from the popular modern worship song "Way Maker" says "even when I can't see it you're working . . . "[11]

And that is definitely the journey I went on with the person who painted the writing on the wall at God's behest, unbeknownst to me at the time. Though knownst (lol) to me when on God's timing, he led me to encounter it.

God had planned in advance where I would be . . . and even aimlessly guided my footsteps and argument with him in front of the house; knowing full well that it pleased him to reveal himself to me as he did. The bigger my argument with him . . . the greater his glory as he proved to me he knew I'd argue with him and he had the painter prepare that paint on the rear wall of the house to silence my objections and strike me dumb with his powerful glory!

Truly, "your word is a lamp to my feet and a light unto my path."[12] In this case, I use the words "your word" more broadly to include the promptings/words from the Holy Spirit in addition to the literal words recorded in the Bible.

Many other times have I wanted God to direct my paths and life choices, so I would simply know for sure which way I should go and then head in that path. And many times, he has remained silent; leaving the proverbial

11. Sinach, *Way Maker*
12. New International Version, *Psalms 119:105*, www.bible.com

choices up to me to make. God is not a magic 8 ball. And I don't think he wants to be used as one. We each have our own free will; and though we are determined (as children of God) to honor him with our life choices; he gives us the free will to choose our direction at all times. For good or ill or rather than "ill", I prefer to use the phrase for our eventual spiritual learning/growth. " . . . for we know that God works all things together for good for those who love him who have been called according to his purpose."[13] Note those qualifiers in that verse too.

I do draw great comfort however; that no matter how murky my path . . . God has had his hand on me and led me through the wilderness to a greater awareness of him, the Holy Spirit and Jesus as a part of my sanctification journey/walk in life.

13. New International Version, *Romans 8:28*, www.bible.com

Chapter 6

Discerning the Voice of the Holy Spirit in Your Life

"Before a word is on my tongue you, Lord, know it completely."[1] — Psalms 139:4

GOD'S SOVEREIGNTY

The Holy Spirit is what leads you to choose Christ.

So whether you are already a christian in your own mind . . . or merely weighing up the "options" so to speak . . . the Holy Spirit is calling to you.

"For many are invited but few are chosen."[2] — Matthew 22:14

If you are truly chosen . . . at some point, you will choose christ/listen to the Holy Spirit; whether that is in your past, present or future.

With or without reading/responding now to what I have to say about discernment here.

But if you are merely 'invited by the Holy Spirit but not chosen'; at some point, you will ignore the Holy Spirit in your heart and ultimately fall away from God permanently (not temporarily like the prodigal son[3] who falls away for a time, comes to his senses and is restored to God); despite coming into contact with God/the Holy Spirit at some point in your life.

So me, trying to teach you what I know here; and you, learning the effectiveness of what I'm saying in practice hence, is partly dependent on

---

1. New International Version, *Psalms 139:4*, www.bible.com
2. New International Version, *Matthew 22:14*, www.bible.com
3. New International Version, Luke 15:11–32, www.bible.com

God and whether you are predestined to believe/choose Christ/listen to the Holy Spirit or whether you are not.

For "God has mercy on whom he wants to have mercy, and he hardens whom he wants to harden."[4]

God is sovereign. Not man. Not you. Not me.

Now, having said that qualifier . . . there are a few tips on discerning the voice of the Holy Spirit that I can give.

TEST THE HOLY SPIRIT

Firstly; if the voice in your head *might* be the holy spirit giving you direction . . . before you listen to it . . . ideally you'd first better be sure it is the Holy Spirit's voice and not your own imaginings of one form or another; also ideally, before you put into practice his instructions. (Test the piece of direction in other words.)

If you use the phrase "the Holy Spirit/God" told me to do x or y . . . Can you present proof that he told you to do x and y to said person you're telling the story to?

I can and have presented proof here — in the writing on the wall; that it was the Holy Spirit telling me to fly to Christchurch . . . and not my own imaginings.

But could I have proved that to anyone else before I left and obeyed the Holy Spirit?

No, I had no immediate proof to offer to anyone (only now, in the aftermath do I have that). But what I could do that was essential to prove that it was the Holy Spirit's voice, I did do in order to prove it . . . And that was to listen to it, obey it but only so *far* as to *make* the Holy Spirit prove himself to me, that it was his voice guiding me and that indeed he had something to teach me on this particular journey about discerning the Holy Spirit . . . And that was in practice, I employed the tried and true scientific method of conduct a test/experiment and quantify/analyze the result to draw an appropriate conclusion.

Has the Holy Spirit proved to you; when he speaks to you, that indeed it was the Holy Spirit speaking and not some other voice/your own thought?

Have you forced the Holy Spirit into a corner . . . where there is no other possible result of your test but that the result, either internally or

4. New International Version, *Romans 9:18*, www.bible.com

externally definitively proves that the direction given came from the Holy Spirit/outside of your own mind and what you could possibly know in and of yourself? (Though that spirit's voice/thought/may have been internal only.)

Essentially I said: "God, I feel you are telling me to fly to Christchurch. And I said I will obey you, so I will go and I will completely listen to all your directions that are a part of this test — that are clearly not sinful and quite possibly are as a result, coming directly from you . . . but at some point I won't listen further to directions if you don't prove to me a point in why you want me to travel there."

That may not have been a direct conscious thought I had at the time; but that was nevertheless the attitude I had beneath my obedience and willingness to go to Christchurch on a "whim" from what I thought was the Holy Spirit. Note also; regarding my night with the apple on the tree . . . I had also had *prior experience* of putting myself "out there in total submissive ways" to the Lord in order to discover what he wanted me to discover . . . My night in Christchurch, was not the first time I had listened to the Holy Spirit with total commitment. Far from. Practice makes perfect they say.

Also, had I flown to Christchurch and received no proof from the Holy Spirit in real world terms (in this case the proof was: the argument/prophecy and immediate fulfillment of it in finding the Writing on the Wall that somehow, impossibly, he had led me to the one house that had that painted on its rear wall amongst the billions of houses in the world); I would not say that it was the Holy Spirit that led me there.

Instead I would be writing a treatise on how my mental illness made me do crazy things and utilized as an example flying to Christchurch on *my own* whim (that clearly wasn't a request of the Holy Spirit judging by my failure to find the back door unlocked and no writing on the wall) and how I merely thought I was having an actual but proven to be merely imaginary argument in my head with "God" that some random house in front of me, would have its back door unlocked and that I had permission to enter the house somehow . . . when in fact I found the backdoor locked and no writing on the rear wall of the house giving me permission to enter. I then came to my senses, realized I had been utterly crazy and insane and promptly flew home and never dared trust another voice in my head again. Result analyzed. Not the Holy Spirit speaking to me. Only my own psychotic imaginings. End of Book.

The whole thing would have been merely me acting deluded and under a psychosis.

Instead, I boldly say *"God* himself" led me there. *God* asked me to travel there. *God* himself argued with me in front of the house concerned and *God* showed me the writing on the wall and how he, *God* had prepared that house in advance for my arrival just to *prove* that it was *God* himself who had been speaking to me. The writing on the wall was *proof* I saw with my own eyes. Verified that it was visible to others as well when the man in the suit, the next morning acknowledged it was there and asked me how did I know about it. So not an illusion. *Proof!!!!*

I do not say *God* told me to cook pork chops for dinner tonight. Where is the proof of that direction coming from *God?*

Without proof it is possibly just a mere delusion that it was God or the Holy Spirit speaking to you. *God* gave me *proof!!!!* Until that moment in front when my actual eyes saw the actual writing on the wall . . . It was merely an experiment. It *might* be God directing me and my footsteps . . . but it *might not* be God too . . . God was testing me — but so too was I testing God and testing myself.

So before I tell you *"God"* told me other stuff . . . or you tell me *"God"* told you to do x or y . . . You better be able to prove that other stuff to me just as I better be able to prove it to you! I'd like my next book to be a compilation of stories from others of how their faith in God has been verified by some form of proof further to this actual point.

And before you think I'm wrenching my shoulder out of it's socket to pat myself on the back for all the things I did do well, to obey, to fully submit, to seek God, to read his word/know him, to pray . . . I'm going to quote a Facebook meme supposedly from Martin Luther "To know Christ and to believe in him is no achievement of man but the gift of God."[5] (I hope he said it — either way, I agree with it) What I do know . . . God has graciously given me. And I share what he has done for me, what I did do well and not so well and my experienced opinion on what you need to do well also, in order to be more receptive to the gift of God in his Holy Spirit . . . rather than be rejecting of it.

5. Wallace, *Facebook News Feed Martin Luther Meme*

TOTAL SUBMISSION

I also held nothing back from God in my heart. I was his completely. I'd even, temporarily, removed my identity as Justin Brent Wallace . . . according to what I felt was part of his test of me.

At every testing step of the way, I aced each step of complete love, obedience, faith, trust and submission. And there were many steps (as the detailed chapters prior to this reveal). I was seeking the Lord fully. Not to please myself. Not to please my fellow man. It was about pleasing God. Not me. I was *His* vessel. But even as I went, I still wouldn't trust the Holy Spirit's direction completely that it was he who had sent me to Christchurch . . . unless he proved it to me beyond all reasonable doubt. And he did that!

You want to test the Lord and so accurately discern that some piece of direction in your head/heart is from him/the Holy Spirit? First make yourself his vessel. Completely. Hold nothing back from him in your love of him. Not your life (which I had already some years before proven that I valued that less, than I valued pleasing him and my love for him). Not your partner. Your job. Possessions. Valued interests. Friends. Family. Life Goals. This is a dangerous book to even suggest you must do that — let alone prove how my doing that was rewarded by God!

Pleasing him is to be your number one goal!

Then, if you believe you truly meet that criteria . . . you can then in doubt even, rather than confidence . . . *Dare* to put that piece of advice you think may be coming from the Holy Spirit to the test. So obey that advice from the Holy Spirit . . . but also commit no sin in so doing.

The Holy Spirit will never ask you to truly sin — though "illegal" is a grey area . . . Do not do anything illegal if at all possible and if asked to do so . . . check again with the Holy Spirit . . . make it give you proof *before* you do anything illegal. You may be required one day as I'm doing right now to prove to 'those chosen' that it is better for you to obey God rather than man[6] (As Peter/John said when questioned by the pharisees in the book of acts) if something the Holy Spirit asks you to do comes into conflict with something that is illegal to do; e.g., Leave Brisbane without telling anyone and later, break and enter. I didn't break the law . . . I sought clarification when God asked me to do something I thought might be illegal; even if it wasn't sin. The writing on the wall gave me proof/permission to enter that

---

6. New International Version, *Acts 5:29*, www.bible.com

abode — so I didn't do anything illegal technically or 'break/enter' — door unlocked — as I had permission.

PROOF/EVIDENCE

And if the result of your dare to put the spirit of God to the test in this brings proof that it was him telling you . . . Hooray, say it, do it, follow it by all means! That proof might even be the point of your travels and way more important than any "destination" or overnight stay in some strange house or actual result of your obedience and submission to God/the holy spirit.

Then you can say, for instance, "God told me to go to Bible College and become a Pastor," and share your proof to those who ask. But if you cannot *prove* it in some way when asked; ("Always be prepared to give an answer to everyone who asks you to give the reason for the hope that you have."[7] This entire book is part of me doing that in practice too) instead merely say "I want to become a Pastor and I hope it is God's will for me to be a pastor and when I graduate, I hope to convince a church to hire me." Do not say "God has called me to become a Pastor," if you cannot present proof that that was God's direction! How? How did God tell you that?

There is a big difference in semantics! And the saying "God told me to do so" is an easily over-used and easily twisted excuse behind what you tell people when you tell them why you are doing what you are doing. State your proof when asked. As I have stated mine here; in either a short synopsis answer which I listed at the beginning of this book or in a more detailed one to people interested like this entire book represents.

I certainly do not say in this book that God has called me to become a Pastor! Instead, I say God called me to Christchurch and showed me that it was him calling because he led me to the writing on the wall. Which presented as scientific, verifiable, visible, actual proof that it was the Holy Spirit guiding me to me. And as a result, I present my proof to you that I can effectively discern the voice of the holy spirit from other voices in my head and that this qualifies me to talk to you now about how to better see the Holy Spirit in life and discern better the Holy Spirit in your head, from your own voice. I dare to present myself as an expert in this; because I am someone who has done this and I have presented my proof to you of having done it. I believe God himself has qualified me, the called, to be a suitable representative to present my experiences and relevant advice on *this* matter.

7. New International Version, *1 Peter 3:15*, www.bible.com

Therefore, you can take my words with confidence, having removed the plank of myself from my eye that I know how to help you better discern the speck in your eye[8] that *might* be preventing you from effectively discerning the holy spirit in your own life.

If I ever say "God has called me to become a Pastor," I will present whatever proof I have from God that it was him calling me to become a Pastor to the person I am telling that story to. And in the meantime, if I ever go to a church for a job as a Pastor, I would merely say, "I would like to be your Pastor." I will present it in just such a way . . . unless I can present proof that God told me to apply for the job. (He certainly has not *given me* such direction or *proof* of that at this time.)

Though I may be an unofficial Pastor in a small way, to a small field of influence through sharing what God has done for me to those who read this or to those I meet who I tell in person . . . in telling the story of the writing on the wall and my subsequent analysis/conclusions . . . but I only share that God has called me to share what God has done for me . . . because it says plainly in the Bible; we are to share what God has done for us![9]

And that speck that prevents you in your own eye from effectively discerning and obeying the Holy Spirit?

Well, as I've said here already . . . it comes back to commitment. Are you fully committed to God? Or do you hold things back in your commitment?

Are you truly seeking the Lord with all your heart in order to find him?[10] For if it is with all your heart and you have already had proof of him — then all I have merely presented here in this story for you, is the story of someone else finding the Lord who has also fully sought him and held nothing back. Something you should be encouraged to find. You aren't the only one who has sought and found him who has experiential "knowledge" of him beyond mere "faith" — by holding nothing back from him as I did.

So you've merely read an inspiring memoir of someone else who fully trusts the Lord . . . and values, like you, nothing other than pleasing him. And what's more . . . God gave him proof that it was the Holy Spirit speaking directly to him! How cool is that!

Such will be your reaction.

But if you try to hold anything back from God . . . God is not fooled. You will *probably not* find proof of him nor discern accurately what the

8. New King James Version, *Luke 6:42*, www.bible.com

9. New International Version, Luke 8:39, www.bible.com

10. New International Version, *Jeremiah 29:13*, www.bible.com

Holy Spirit is trying to show you or say to you. And you will only find the evidence you *wish* to see from any tests you conduct as well . . . the true discernment/piece of evidence that it was God giving you that piece of direction will likely elude you . . . instead you will always wonder . . . Was it merely myself . . . or even some other form of spirit/demon whispering to me whose advice I followed in situation x or y . . .

PRAY

But if you say to me, you have held nothing back in your commitment to him . . . You live and die wholly for the Lord . . . what else do I need to do to detect that difference between his voice and my own or other's voices in my mind . . . You are either lying or God himself will provide the direction through circumstance that you are seeking.

Unsure of which job to take when there are two offers on the table? Feel like you're fully committed to the Lord . . . but the merits of both jobs seem equal . . . and you just can't decide?

Pray! I was praying in my head, throughout my journey to Christchurch and travel there before I found the house with the writing on the wall. I had a 48 hour intermittent, casual, prayer session with God as I walked.

Be in communion with God. Talk to him in your head. Like thoughts. Try to imagine what advice God might offer you in your 'imaginary' conversation with God. You might just find that that imaginary conversation becomes an actual conversation with God . . . like I was having in front of the house with the writing on the wall.

KNOW GOD'S CHARACTER

To try falling asleep, you must first start to act as if you are asleep. To try hearing from God; sometimes you must first act as if that imaginary voice in your head, is the actual voice of God . . . and then, have a conversation yourself with him in your mind. But do you know God's character well enough however? Have you already spent years meditating on his word, as I had, to even form a somewhat accurate opinion of what his view on my situation might be? Can you actually conceive what he might say were he another person standing in the room with you and be accurate? So if you asked him for his opinion in order to even have a remotely accurate imaginary conversation with him in your head, let alone a non-imaginary one . . . to even begin to discern the difference between actual and imaginary? The more you know God. The more you read his word . . . the more you'll know what his opinion is on your circumstance.

If the "direction" in your imaginary conversation leads you to sin . . . it's not an actual conversation with God — merely an imaginary one. *But if the conversation provides proof that it is from God . . .* follow that direction and praise God for the proof and the input he has deigned to have upon the choice that yet lies before you! Any proof he has given me is for his glory and his glory alone. I'm certainly not worthy of any — as the chapter Confession time proves.

"What is mankind that you are mindful of them, human beings that you care for them?"[11]

Further — I am extremely humbled — that the God of the galaxy . . . chose to have a scientifically proven actual conversation with me in my head! Little ol' me! And he wants to converse with you too — if you dare! It may have started as a scientifically testing imaginary conversation but he proved it was real when he led me to stand in front of the house with the Writing on the Wall 48 hours later! I certainly read Psalms 139[12] with fresh eyes after this event. I'd encourage each of you to read that entire Psalm as well for a better understanding of what I mean here.

I'm certainly not saying every "imaginary conversation" I have in my head is actually God speaking to me. Far from! But if it is God — in some way; there will be some proof of this or evidence of this — and he gave that to me on *that* occasion.

Also, the advice will never *contradict* the character of God that we know from his word/Bible. Though it may be counter-intuitive; e.g., God may ask you to do something "man" may think is foolish. To step out in faith and trust him. That is ok.

I have imaginary conversations in my head quite often. I rehearse conversations with people I know. People I want to know better. People I wish I knew. People I don't want to know. And God as I present my cares and concerns to him. If evidence is presented that it is undoubtedly God talking back to you — *Great!* Share that! That's certainly what I've done here!

I also had to have a fairly good idea of God's character to even begin to imagine that what he might say to me in an imaginary conversation, would

11. New International Version, *Psalms 8:4*, www.bible.com
12. New International Version, *Psalms 139*, www.bible.com

in fact be in keeping with the character of God that I know from years of Bible study prior.

Though that doesn't mean that God necessitates us to have done years of Bible study in order to know him. God reveals himself to people in life, for his reasons, in his ways. Once the characters in the Bible . . . didn't have a Bible to get to know God . . . God revealed himself and his character to them through his Holy Spirit and proved his presence to them as well in the examples in the Bible stories. Knowing God's character beforehand will help guide you . . . but like anything with God . . . if he chooses to act without that prerequisite/advice already present in your life, that sovereignty/prerogative is forever his to determine.

Is there a different feel to the voice of the Holy Spirit and your own thoughts? Did I experience that? In some ways, sorry to disappoint you — but the thoughts I felt were as similar as if I were the author of both what I thought I was saying and what I thought/imagined what God was saying in reply.

But the Writing on the Wall — proved to me, that I was not the author of all that I thought could have been my own voice 'acting' as the voice of God. That it was in fact the Holy Spirit's voice I was conversing with at that time.

Is there evidence? Is there a definitive answer? Be scientific as I was, in your own testing and imaginary conversations with God. I'll reference Gideon's fleece wet and dry test here.[13] Gideon asked God to prove that it was God's Holy Spirit speaking to him and then proof of that is detailed in that chapter. If it is really God speaking to you; he will present some form of evidence that you will accept as proof that it was God speaking to you. As the writing on the wall was proof to me, that it was God speaking to me in front of that house.

So if the feeling is the same, how can I better discern my voice from God's voice?

The proof is in the pudding. Listen. Pray. Submit. Obey God. Know God's character; through his word and apply it. To ask again . . . To state this another way . . . How well do you think I knew God's character before the writing on the wall? I had read the Bible cover to cover — many times . . . I knew what was in his character in each thought I had as I journeyed with him for 48 hours to Christchurch and which thoughts were clearly not in his character and were merely my own. Of myself, I had spent years in

13. New International Version, *Judges 6*, www.bible.com

a sanctifying walk with the Lord; beyond my mere salvation/justification/conversion to the faith. And if you think you can accurately discern the same and there is still no evidence that that voice in your head is God — then in all likelihood it is either not God — or God has simply chosen not to provide you with definitive proof for the time being. He provided me with definitive proof 48 hours later . . . not that night in Brisbane, I had to obey and put him to the test *first* too . . . but he doesn't always provide me with proof.

Sometimes, because of his immutable ways; does not the potter have the right to make what he will of the clay . . . [14] or Where were you when he laid the foundations of the earth?[15] . . . the answer will not be plainly given. And we are subject to his will. He is not our genie, subject to giving us all we want. We are his subjects. If the answer is silence; then it may be he is leaving the choice of which job to take, all things being equal, purely up to you and he wants that choice to be yours and yours alone — or to consider other factors. Other times, he may intervene.

I praise him for his intervention that night I stood outside that house in Christchurch.

The God of the Galaxy chose to tell me he had prepared in advance for my arrival there.

How humbling and beautiful and caring is that?

And if he cares for me, the least of his children (My confessions only touch the surface of my sins of course — again I do not wish to double the length of this book) . . . he cares for you too!

And I hope you find that encouraging!

And I hope that encourages you to both read his word and listen for what may be his Holy Spirit speaking to you that little bit more after reading this book. Yes, it may be merely through having you start an imaginary conversation with God — but it may prove itself to be a real one in time too.

And if that happens . . . if in any small way, I have bolstered your faith in God; that you have found a little more hope in him . . . a little more love in him . . . and a little more confidence in him to make him that much more the Lord of Your life . . . then I am immensely humbled and thrilled to have been of service to you in my attempt, truly, to simply be of service to God, out of gratitude for what he has done for me. Not to secure my salvation . . . for that is found in Jesus alone; his free gift — I cannot earn that; but simply

14. New International Version, *Romans 9:20–21*, www.bible.com

15. New International Version, *Job 38:4*, www.bible.com

out of the overflow of joy in my heart and responsibility I feel to share what God has done for me with others.

Also, in my conversation with God in front of the house; he proved to me that the writing on the wall . . . and the permission I sought from the owner before entering was important. He proved Psalms 139:4 to me. That he knew I would ask for permission by getting someone to paint the writing on the wall well in advance of my arrival to give me that permission. "Before a word is on my tongue, you, Lord, know it completely."[16]

And he delighted to prove that to me.

To God be the Glory!

What more proof do you require in order to believe in God? To know God. To read his word. To obey God? To try to listen more to the Holy Spirit speaking to you? To submit to God? That God loves you? That God is worthy of praise?

This is a book that tries to present proof of God — through how his Holy Spirit works — rather than use a more traditional apologetic stance through arguing God's exists because of Creation; that evolution is clearly false or through even using the ten commandments to show how fallen we are and how Holy God is and presenting our need for a savior. All these approaches of course have their merits.

I have taken a different "apologetic" approach in the defense of the faith, so to speak in this book. I present my experiences here. And show how God has worked through my experiences to prove himself beyond doubt to me that he exists and that he talks directly to me in my mind as being the reason for the hope that I have in Christ/salvation. I hope this particular approach convinces any skeptics reading this work to believe in God and to listen more to the calling of his Holy Spirit inside them. But the result of that is up to God. You cannot lead a horse to drink. Only to water. Jesus presented himself as living water (and the bread of life[17]); to those who eat and drink; they will be satisfied.[18]

GOD'S LOVE LANGUAGE

Today at church on Christmas Eve, the Senior Pastor Garry Toms of my local Greenslopes Baptist Church made a number of points about our love

16. New International Version, *Psalms 139:4*, www.bible.com

17. New King James Version, *John 6:48–51*, www.bible.com

18. New King James Version, *John 4:14*, www.bible.com

languages and God's love language and how if we speak in the love language of the other person; we reach them, rather than just speaking in whatever love language works best for you personally.

He said when we speak God's love language to him, we open ourselves up to receiving his blessing of himself . . . when we exercise:

"One: Humility; Two: Honesty and Transparency; Three: Risk all we are and have; Four: Persevere; Five: Make God our first priority; and Six: Forgive."[19]

Before I go on to talk about the nature of the Holy Spirit in the final chapter, let me ask you this question:

Did I do all six things first in order for God to then reveal himself to me and reward me with proof that I had effectively discerned the voice of his Holy Spirit at the writing on the wall?

Was I humble? Attempting to please God rather than myself and allow him to choose my direction rather than insist proudly on putting my point of view forward that his direction was crazy and there was no way I was going to fly to Christchurch?

Was I honest and transparent? Have I been anything but in this story? I was clearly not afraid to boldly declare my willingness to make what might seem foolish decisions to mankind (to drop everything and fly to Christchurch); if I felt God had asked me to make them? Did God use that to show what might be foolishness to man, is in fact, the very wisdom of God?[20] Did I not prove, that rather than fear man's ridicule . . . I feared God[21], so I would do what I felt he might be asking me to do . . . even as I put that idea to the test.

Did I risk all I am for him and him alone? Absolutely. I proved that in the life-test if not in being willing to drop my life in Brisbane, spend all the little money I had at that point and simply fly to Christchurch, simply because I felt him ask me to. And damn the consequences.

Did I persevere or demand instant results or to know why before going to Christchurch? Yes, I persevered for years in my trust of him . . . before and between returning the apple to the tree and finding the writing on the wall. And when I felt the call from him come 30 years into my faith journey, I just went . . . and obeyed and persevered . . . throughout the 48 hour journey until I felt it had reached its end and I did, understandably I feel,

19. Toms, *24th December 2023 Sermon*
20. New King James Version, *1 Corinthians 3:19*, www.bible.com
21. New International Version, *Proverbs 9:10*, www.bible.com

eventually lose my patience and I challenged God to give me the point . . . at the exact point, he knew I would lose patience with him and challenge him.

Did I make God my first priority? Unarguable.

Did I show that I had to learn to forgive others and myself . . . not to judge them unjustly? I believe I did — in returning the apple to the tree — even though forgiving other's sins towards me is not the exact focus of this book. Forgiveness is important of course. There are many parables and points in the Bible surrounding unforgiveness and God *may* withhold forgiveness[22] if we aren't able to forgive others. Even the Lord's prayer has a strong forgiveness focus. We pray the Lord will forgive us our sins even as we forgive those who sin against us.[23] Though I do recognize; forgiveness sometimes is a process; more on that soon in the section under trauma.

Therefore, I opened myself up to receiving God himself . . . the object of my love . . . and also went on to learn through my subsequent confessions that God speaks the truth in love[24] to me . . . and in so doing . . . he rebuked my twisting of christian liberty . . . and helped me remove the plank from my eye[25], so I could better help you with the speck of learning how to better trust him completely and submit to and discern better the voice of the Holy Spirit speaking inside you.

I was rewarded with greater knowledge and faith and trust in him. And when you submit to the Holy Spirit speaking to you, so too, you will be rewarded with what truly matters. Him.

A NOTE ON TRAUMA AND SIN

If all other things I've talked about here are equal . . . It is entirely possible, because of past trauma and sin's consequences alone that you are unable to effectively see the Holy Spirit in life and so discern the Holy Spirit's voice inside your mind. Even if you are fully committed to God and know his character well. The Holy Spirit is aware of this but the responsibility is not on him alone for you to deal with your trauma. The Holy Spirit will want to help you to deal with your trauma and lead you away from sin of course — but it is possible, given the nature of your trauma that you need to seek external counseling of one form or another. For I believe, while you're

22. New International Version, *Matthew 7:1–5*, www.bible.com
23. New International Version, *Luke 11:4*, www.bible.com
24. New International Version, *Ephesians 4:15*, www.bible.com
25. New International Version, *Matthew 7:5*, www.bible.com

brave enough to look at your issues, the Holy Spirit will be at the same time attempting to help you understand and overcome those issues and their effects on your thoughts, attitudes and behaviors. Sin and Trauma's consequences can take a lifetime to understand, manage and move beyond. Indeed any progress at all should be cause to praise God for his grace in helping you through them in whatever manner is helpful.

Some personal trauma issues are complex and you should not expect to be able to clearly discern the Holy Spirit's voice from your own negative voices, or even that of your parents' (for instance) ingrained voices in your head if you have not effectively moved on in your life and inner thought attitudes, beyond their potentially negative consequences.

For myself to effectively discern the Holy Spirit's voice from my own "trauma voice" — I had to move beyond relational trauma created by my parent's divorce when I was young as well as my own divorce just a few years before I returned the apple to the tree.

Have you forgiven your father for any unfortunate behavior when you were a child? I have. Truly. I enjoy as good a relationship now with him, as practical, under our life's circumstances. To me the past is a non-issue. As an adult, I understand better his motivations and his weaknesses and certainly have had some of the same myself; for good or ill. I have also come to admire him for his strengths.

Have you forgiven your ex-wife for leaving you? I have.

Have you forgiven yourself for any unfortunate things you did to contribute to her leaving? I have.

Do you relate to others based purely on those relationships and not with the scars from previous failed relationship attempts with anyone? I certainly do this to the best of my ability, though of course, like anyone, I am not perfect at this.

Therefore, I am doing my practical best to not let trauma get in the way in my attempts to effectively discern the Holy Spirit's voice inside me; hearing that voice, testing it and then in obedience, following it's wisdom/ guidance/direction in my life/choices.

It is the same with sin. I'm going to quote the esteemed reformed modern preacher Paul Washer from an internet meme (I hope he said it — either way, I agree with it).

"The mark of the true believer is not sinless perfection, but new repugnance for sin, a greater sensitivity to sin, a more vehement zeal to fight against sin, a humble contrition because of sin, and a willingness to confess sin."[26]

If these 6 things are in your genuine attitude; then you are doing your best through the work of the Holy Spirit to combat your sin and at the same time you should be more open to the Holy Spirit's promptings to further move beyond your sin and clearly discern his voice/presence better in your life.

Have I not shown here my own willingness to confess my sin and my desire to fight against my own sin as well as a genuine repugnance for it and even a humble contrition of it? I'm not proud of my flaws and I want to cut them out of my life as much as possible.

If/when you can say the same; you'll have moved beyond the potentially devastating effects of both yours/others sin and the result trauma can have on accurately discerning the Holy Spirit's voice inside you and hopefully you'll be at an emotional, stable place where you are much more receptive and obedient to following the Holy Spirit's direction in your life too.

How did I move beyond my own personal trauma? What works for me; is a simple answer that I understand may not work for others. Forgiveness of others, myself and faith in the Lord; that although I remain a sinner, and know others are too; that God wants us to have faith in him and learn from our prior experiences. Most importantly — Don't let yours or others sin get in the way of your relationship with God — and where practical — your relationships with other people too. To me, everything is like an experiment. Treating my ex-wife poorly, with a lack of patience at the back end of our relationship, clearly didn't work! So, I analyze and learn. For instance, I show more patience with people in the present, (rather than the past which I cannot control) and that more patience means, new people relate better to me and I find myself in less aggravating arguments for instance than I did when I was in my early 20s.

I wish each of you all the best in your inner walk with the Holy Spirit as we each hopefully learn the lessons we need to learn from each day we live.

Having said all that I've said in this chapter, however, perfection is not a requirement this side of heaven. That means, you may still be able to effectively discern the voice of the Holy Spirit in your mind and see him in your life even if you haven't dealt with all your trauma, aren't fully committed,

26. Wallace, *Facebook News Feed Paul Washer Meme*

are pretty disobedient, don't know God's character well and you remain determined to go in no direction but your own in life.

Which, I find encouraging, despite the mess we may find ourselves in. The spirit of God is calling you. I hope you listen to what he is trying to say to you. But it is more likely, if you are disobedient, that you will not likely be able to clearly discern the voice of the Holy Spirit in your life.

Therefore, while you don't have to be perfect, you really should be open to removing what you see as sin from your life as much as possible and putting into practice the good works that are the fruit of a genuine faith in God.[27]

Galatians 5:16 says "If you are guided by the spirit, you won't obey your selfish desires."[28]

Oh, if only I was always purely obedient and submissive to the truth in that verse! When I have been responsive to and guided by the spirit, has been the only way I've achieved genuine success/self-control over those sinful practices and desires and when I have not been . . . has been when I've gotten myself into trouble! This is why this book is so important and making/emphasizing why it is so important to discern the voice of the Holy Spirit! Only when we do discern clearly the voice of the Holy Spirit — can we truly walk deeper down the path of sanctification towards pleasing God. Spiritual meat! As opposed to the spiritual milk of a conversion/justification by faith alone gospel.[29]

The Holy Spirit is there, inside you, wanting to make you more Christlike and any refusal, whether obvious or subtle to his promptings to either remove sin or act in a way where you feel he is prompting you to act, will interfere with your future ability to clearly discern his voice and submit to his guidance in your life. And thereby prevent you from showing the spiritual fruit that proves your faith in God is genuine.[30]

Without going into great detail; there have been hundreds of occasions where I've felt the Holy Spirit prompt me to start speaking to someone new for instance, and on many of those occasions, I've deliberately disobeyed and ignored the spirit; writing it off as crazy or simply as something I don't want to do. Why should I go talk to a stranger? I'm happy as I am.

---

27. New King James Version, *James 2:14–26*, www.bible.com

28. Contemporary English Version, *Galatians 5:16*, www.bible.com

29. New International Version, *Romans 2:8*, www.bible.com

30. New International Version, *James 2:26*, www.bible.com

But am I being obedient in such a response? Am I being submissive? Do I even know for sure that it was the Holy Spirit prompting me to start a conversation that never happened? All, I know is, that my own submission and obedience is a daily work in progress. It is likely I or they missed out on further blessings when I ignored the Holy Spirit's promptings . . . But being receptive to the spirit; I knew in my own conscience I was being disobedient and I know in my future, I need to listen better, be more discerning and more obedient than I have been in the past.

I do desire to please God. Yet so often, I write off the Holy Spirit's prompts as crazy . . . like hearing advice in an earpiece from a friend to say to someone else in a conversation, "I feel God would like me to talk to you right now . . . but I just don't know why. Maybe I'm wrong. Would you like to chat to me for a few moments and see how we connect?" The awkward/honest words stick in my throat and I refuse to obey. Such a conversation starter seems so bold and even as a ridiculous way to start a conversation with someone, that so often I fail to do this . . . and ignore the spirit's promptings. Instead in my mind I say "No God, I'm not saying that. I'm not doing that. I'm just going to go my way."

I hope this book has prompted you to obey more of the spirit's promptings in future. No matter how crazy the prompting may make you feel. It's only personal ego/pride at times that prevents us from humbly revealing that it might just be the Holy Spirit prompting us to start a conversation with a stranger at church. And is that pride a good thing? You know the answer to that.

Finally, (for this chapter) I want to reiterate on an idea I touched briefly upon earlier. I believe that the Holy Spirit can speak to us as a result of the stimuli that comes into our awareness. Whether that is, for example, through a passing billboard with the word "Eternity" which might indicate a fragrance brand in the advertisement but in the Holy Spirit's prompts could be a gentle reminder to see his presence in the real world. Will you simply see the literal fragrance advertisement; or will you see it as a subtle reminder perhaps of the Holy Spirit attempting to get your attention?

Naturally, as I've already said, I see the literal/lateral and the concrete/abstract often; so I see God's hand in what appeals to human nature to merely sell a perfume. Why our nature is even attracted to such a spiritual word as eternity and even consider associating that with God/the Holy Spirit. I hope after you've read everything I've said here that you too will be more open in your spirit to seeing God's spirit at work in the world. I can barely watch any tv ad for instance and not find some form of spiritual connotation in it. Once you open your eyes to this I believe; you too will see the same.

Chapter 7

The Nature of the Holy Spirit

"If you are guided by the Spirit, you won't obey your selfish desires."[1]
— Galatians 5:16

HOLINESS

If there is one section in what I'm writing on how to discern the Holy Spirit's voice speaking to you in order to better see the Holy Spirit in life that might be tough for me to give my opinion on and yet stay completely theologically, fundamentally correct in every way; it is this one.

So please don't twist in your own interpretations what I am saying in this section into something I am not saying. For it may be easy for you to do that. Just don't. All right. ;)

What isn't controversial is that the Holy Spirit's nature is Holy and inwardly guides us to perfect us and help us become more holy, Christ-like and sanctified. Bringing to our attention our flaws and areas in our life where we can make such improvements in our attitudes and behavior and hence become more Christ-like.

What may be controversial is for me to suggest that the Holy Spirit can also speak to us and give us information we have no other ways or means of knowing. WHEN it is through the spirit only that you know what you know. Whether that is what someone else may be saying, thinking, doing or feeling . . . who is outside you or some form of circumstantial knowledge.

---

1. Contemporary English Version, *Galatians 5:16*, www.bible.com

God the father is omnipotent, God the son is in perfect union with God the father and when God the father wishes it, he will through the Holy Spirit give Jesus knowledge that Jesus has no other source of knowing and because they are in perfect union; Jesus will know and not doubt that it is true. Hence, Jesus knew in his spirit that the pharisees were thinking awful things of him, when they were testing him at times in the gospels. The Bible indicates he knew in his spirit exactly what they were thinking in their spirits.[234] These 3 footnotes indicate 3 examples of this.

DIRECT KNOWLEDGE

With that omnipotence, direct knowledge (not special 'revelation' e.g., adding to scripture with new ideas that are not scriptural) *may* come through the Holy Spirit at times of exactly what others may be thinking, saying or doing . . . even when you have no other source of knowing that. To quote Harry Potter's accusation of Malfoy of being the one who cursed Katie Bell; despite a lack of evidence. "It was Malfoy! I know it!" Harry did just know. And Harry was right.[5]

Yet on many such occasions this circumstance of "just knowing" in life is written off by many as purely "coincidental" . . . It was only an accident of competing and comparative probabilities combined with internal deductive reasoning should your "hunch", later prove correct. Maybe large odds or small of it happening. And using this idea across all examples in your life, the evidence of "God" is hence easily discarded as not providing enough proof or evidence, hence of the Holy Spirit's voice acting in some way inside you.

To quote the movie, The Mummy Returns just for fun, "My friend, there is a fine line between coincidence and fate."[6]

I think there are no coincidences. There is the Holy Spirit and what may be other spirits attempting to impart knowledge too. Lying spirits. Demonic Spirits. But if you have been led into "truth" in some form; I would argue that that "truth" is the proof that it was the Holy Spirit imparting that piece of knowledge to you.

2. New International Version, *Luke 5:22*, www.bible.com

3. New International Version, *Luke 6:8*, www.bible.com

4. New International Version, *Mark 2:8*, www.bible.com

5. Yates, *Harry Potter and the Half-Blood Prince*

6. Sommers, *The Mummy Returns*

If you are looking for evidence of God . . . I think you need look no further than how the Holy Spirit is attempting to communicate with you in your own mind and heart. (If indeed creation itself is not proof enough for you!)

Of course, the Holy Spirit imparted to me, truth, knowledge I had no other way of knowing when he said to me I would find the back door of the house unlocked and that I would have the owner's permission, if I simply put him to the test and walked down that driveway . . . He told me the truth . . . and fortunately was amused enough with me to allow me to put him to that test. There are hundreds of thousands of houses I could have knocked on instead in that city . . . That 'direct' knowledge was imparted to me by the Holy Spirit. Opening the unlocked back door and reading the writing on the wall, was merely me encountering proof that the Holy Spirit had not lied to me but had told me the truth.

For lying spirits want to lead you away from God and faith in him as the author of creation and indeed any of the stuff easily labelled as the supernatural . . . those spirits do not want to lead you closer to him. Which is of course one reason why Satan wants to hide his existence. He doesn't want to create faith in those who would see his very existence as proof of God's existence and hence leave you feeling you have no option but to repent of your sin and devote your life to God. (Which is of course what I'm doing anyway) So, too is it with the other just as real demons.

To put it another way, this potentially controversial idea I'm talking about here is kind of like the concept of a hive mind . . . except what I'm saying is we each have a hive spirit, living in each of us, called the Holy Spirit. Some will heed the spirit's inclinations and voice and find life . . . others rebel against the spirit unto death. Indeed the unforgivable sin, seems to imply in context that it is attributing to the Holy Spirit, evil works. Which can in the end, only be a complete and utter tuning out of the Holy Spirit in your mind/heart and labelling his inclinations hence as utter foolishness, so you don't follow them. So you'll miss out on the eternal life made possible through the spirit living in us and everlasting forgiveness through Jesus and permanently restored relationship with God the father that was fractured in the Garden of Eden.

At times, whether they be frequent or rare in some people; the Holy Spirit may illumine that person into knowing something, they have no other direct means of knowing. Whether that something is imparting knowledge of God's character who, then, inspired, writes it down and it eventually becomes a piece of accepted inspired Scripture canon . . . (Was Moses in the Garden of Eden? Most commentators attribute the creation account to him through his effective discernment of the Holy Spirit's voice telling him what to write.) Or whether that something you have no other way of knowing is through the Holy Spirit giving you the words to say or information about a scenario; like a sixth sense, you have no other way of effectively discerning.

When any of these scenarios occur . . . and it is proven, as I have emphasized elsewhere, in some way to be authored by the Holy Spirit to you — rejoice! The spirit has imparted its wisdom in some way to you . . . but also be humbled . . . for the Holy Spirit felt the need to intervene and there was no other way to impart practically what was imparted to you. For God himself is a mystery to us, as we are in our fallen state and we need him; through his word and spirit to show us himself.

It is also difficult to be guided by the spirit to avoid sin . . . if you do your best to avoid being guided by the spirit!

In this as well, I'd like to comment on offhand "signs". The Holy Spirit may guide in any way . . . and if you are open to seeing it . . . then you will see God everywhere, like I do.

So, recognize when the Holy Spirit has imparted some information to you; for his purposes in refining you or helping you relate to others and give credit to the spirit of God who has done that. So, see it as God at work in you or the situation; rather than writing it off as a mere coincidence, luck or patting your own shoulder on the back in praise of yourself for simply taking advantage of the opportunity before you whenever it supposedly 'fortuitously' presents itself.

That Holy Spirit imparted 'information' might be as simple as some answer/Bible verse dredged up from the deep recesses of your memory that effectively "gives the reason for the hope that you have"[7] when you are talking to a non-christian about why you believe. (It's certainly happened to me many times in the writing of this book.)

This special knowledge, just for you, might also be something you had no other way of knowing at all; that when you act on it; you receive all the proof and verification you need, to know that that impulse or thought, came from the Holy Spirit. For example; to say to someone: "I felt God tell me to knock on your door and ask if you're all right"; to a complete stranger who unbeknownst to him, just happened to be contemplating suicide. (This is a situation that a personal friend of mine related to me from his experience.)

7. New International Version, 1 *Peter 3:15*, www.bible.com

This man was so grateful for the unexpected Holy Spirit timed intervention/knock on his door by a complete stranger; that he went to church for the first time in years the next day; believed in Jesus and repented of what he saw as his sin and in so doing made him the Lord of his life shortly after. Someone else's obedience to the Holy Spirit resulted in the return of a lost sheep/prodigal! Praise God!

So, in such a way, I believe we all have access to the omnipotent hive mind of God through his Holy Spirit inside us. But don't twist that into saying you know what he hasn't said to you. Do the results show proof? That man's suicide was averted. I found the writing on the wall. God will only reveal elements of his omnipotence through his spirit to our finite limited awareness/consciousness for his reasons and on his timing alone. Certainly not according to our own 'command' that he do so. He is not your servant. You are his.

NO COINCIDENCE

As for astrology — I believe it is composed of elements of lying spirits attempt to impart truths to lead people astray or keep them astray. Have nothing to do with it personally but if you find yourself debating with an astrologer — present the Holy Spirit as the only real author of truth . . . for "The heavens declare the glory of God; And the firmament shows His handiwork."[8]

If you see truth in the stars . . . instead of perhaps seeing an unknowable God . . . see the truth of how his Holy Spirit has been attempting to reach you. For any actual truth "the stars" may impart are from him and any lies the stars supposedly impart disguised as "truth" are from the devil's minions.

The number of times, the Holy Spirit has imparted some piece of relevant knowledge or direction to me; that I have either immediately or later known was correct; has been many. But again, I don't always listen it to either.

Just yesterday I was thinking about whether I should invite a friend "Mel" to coffee as I was driving and then a car pulls in front of me with the number plate "Mel" immediately *after* I had this thought. (Obviously it means something entirely different if it was *before*) Clearly the spirit approved of my thought and God the father brought the car into my eye-line

8. New King James Version, *Psalms 19:1*, www.bible.com

THE NATURE OF THE HOLY SPIRIT

to potentially emphasize that as a form of providence. I see God at work. Not a coincidence where I refuse to see God at work and so stick my head in the sand to the possibilities of the Holy Spirit influencing my life.

Here are two more examples of God's Holy Spirit giving me visions/directions. Just to utilize other illustrations/show my testing beyond the writing on the wall and returning the apple to the tree from my life.

SAME PLACE/SAME TIME VISIONS

Firstly, there was this girl I had a crush on for a short time. I knew she was studying at the same Bible college I was at and that she often walked to a class on a particular day, down the long public street before the college. I had driven past her walking before near the obvious start time; through simple good deduction.

Now, as I knew on a given day of our different classes with a similar start time to mine, I thought to myself an hour before I left, a random, scattered thought of her . . . that I might see her walking on my drive to class. But then I had this sudden sense from the Holy Spirit — this exact certainty — that that afternoon, I would see her and give her a ride for the last mile or so of the journey. I had a vision in my head of the exact point on the road I would see her and I felt the spirit tell me with absolute certainty . . . that she would be at that point when I drove near her.

This was a couple of years before returning the apple to the tree but I was nonetheless in my spirit open to the Holy Spirit, testing it, though perhaps my obedience to it was still somewhat reluctant. (And it still isn't at times I wonder?)

Anyway, a rebellious part of my mind immediately responded to that vision by saying . . . right . . . if this vision is really from you Lord . . . I'm going to be ten minutes late to class . . . just to make sure it doesn't happen. What are the chances of her also being ten minutes late? Pretty good as it turns out as I drove up to her in my car at the exact point, an hour later (I had the vision an hour before it came true) on the road where my vision saw she would be.

I picked her up and drove her the final mile to the college's car park. Naturally, I said nothing to her about having a vision of seeing her there — that was between me and the Holy Spirit at that point; merely telling her I'd noticed her walking to class in the past and thought she could use a ride as she was clearly running late, like me.

77

She gratefully accepted it — and smoothly moved on and also out of my life.

My point is not that I was obedient to God's vision . . . God gave me a vision and it came true . . . despite my best efforts for it not to; with the provision that I was still obedient to it . . . I just increased the odds to make it clearer that it had in fact come from the Holy Spirit.

In the past before that, I had shared about and been misunderstood about a previous vision brought on by the Holy Spirit with someone and I was reluctant to share information as a result; for some time regarding the Holy Spirit's visions that have come true for me.

Does that mean all the visions I've had that I thought *might* be from the Holy Spirit came true? No! I am no prophet! But when I've put him to the test . . . when I've engaged with the Holy Spirit . . . then yes, the Holy Spirit has *proved* many to me, though not all. Those that went unproven . . . I think went unproven because I was seeking the power of the Holy Spirit for myself . . . to feel important . . . that if my visions came true . . . then I was someone special . . . But they clearly weren't from the Holy Spirit. They were merely my imagination that they *might* be visions or callings in some way from the Holy Spirit. They were lacking the necessary proof/fulfillment. To say it again. I don't repeat myself. Much! Lol!

If you too, are seeking the Holy Spirit's power — for power's sake . . . it is likely those visions or promptings you have that *might* be from the Holy Spirit . . . are not. But if you are open to his guidance and his direction, fully submissive, know God's character and are seeking to do his will . . . then the guidance you think you *might* be receiving from the Holy Spirit will be proven in some way if it is from him. Whether that is from a stranger knocking on your door offering help in a moment of need . . . or simply arriving at a place at the exact point in time you had a vision of someone else specific arriving at that exact time as well.

Which was also my second vision/example here . . . I had pre-determined to tell Tim (who I dedicated this book to) about my experience in Christchurch as part of a Christmas Card letter . . . and on the drive to his church on Christmas morning, I suddenly worried about the size of the card and getting it squashed in my pocket as well as finding him in the large crowd. I only had one card to give out that morning. To him. "Not to worry", I felt the Holy Spirit respond, "he'll be at the door and you can hand it in person to him then and there." Now Tim was pretty busy . . . being the pastor of a very large megachurch on Christmas morning. A part of me doubted this vision . . . surely he'd be somewhere deeper inside (as I was also running slightly late) but as I approached the entrance to the large foyer, Tim was walking through it. I called out his name; partly in shock, at yet another vision coming true . . . Yeah, you'd think after all this time, I wouldn't still get a sense of shock or wonder . . . but I do every time . . . Tim responded with a greeting and I gave him the card and continued on into the church . . . Once again humbled by the Holy Spirit and needing God's forgiveness yet again for doubting the vision he'd given me as I drove to church that morning.

These things . . . are for God's glory. Not mine. Not yours. The Holy Spirit is not your genie. He is trying to perfect you but also guide you to where you need to be in life. Even if that place is the mechanic's when your car needs to be towed . . . so you can present a positive attitude into what might be a sad situation in a car accident that that mechanic will look at you and marvel. "I'll have what she's having!"[9] (Thanks When Harry Met Sally!) Then you have truly lived Job's mantra . . . "Shall we accept good from God and not trouble . . . "[10] and "The Lord gave and the Lord has taken away; may the name of the Lord be praised."[11]

Or to quote Rudyard Kipling's poem "If": "If you can meet with triumph and disaster and treat those two imposters just the same . . . . . . you'll be a man, my son."[12]

If only I didn't doubt so much the spirit; resist the spirit so much and simply obeyed all the time. Truly, even though I am a man of faith . . . I remain at times, a man of little faith . . .

However, now that I am "looking" and "listening" . . . I am no longer "blind" and "see" and "hear" God everywhere. And I hope you see him a little more everywhere too after reading what I've said in this book.

PROVIDENCE

So, you see God now everywhere. You are receptive to the Holy Spirit's voice and you can discern it clearly from the other voices/thoughts in your head . . . Most of the time. However do you make a mistake now and see him where he isn't? That is always a big question for me and if you see him

9. Reiner, *When Harry Met Sally*
10. New International Version, *Job 2:10*, www.bible.com
11. New International Version, *Job 1:21*, www.bible.com
12. Kipling, *If*

in every speck of coincidence too . . . you may start to see his guidance where it isn't too.

For certainly God provides and guides. And your spirit's acknowledgement of this in his leading of you to a certain place in time where a spine tingling "coincidence" occurs that you feel can only be God's guidance is great . . . But has God provided all of these however? I'm sorry to put a dampener on the "it's not a coincidence it's actually God parade" but the answer is it is extremely unlikely.

I've no doubt he's provided some to you and yes, that is part of his providence/Holy Spirit guidance and it's good for you to acknowledge the part he's had to play in those. However, it is virtually impossible to live a life without encountering coincidence at some level at some point. Are all of those God's attempts to lead you?

I would say, far from. Indeed, many "signs" we see may be of the devil/ rebellious in nature; temptations to lead us astray. We are undoubtedly creatures of suggestion. It is without doubt the main reason why advertising is so effective. To see "holy" significance in every impression/sign we are confronted with is to ignore our very fallen nature and its desire to worship what it sees . . . rather than the unseen through faith. Many of our flaws arise from this element inside our fallen selves. So as much as you wish in every circumstance/sign to see God at work . . . you *must* realize that many of these signs are merely proof of your sinful nature at work instead. And there is a battle that you must fight going on inside you against the desire to twist the image/coincidence before your eyes. To say it is from God . . . when it in most situations is probably more an indicator of your sin/others' sins . . .

The only real tip I have for accurate discernment of such signs is that the proof is in the pudding. If the result, brings you closer to God . . . then for whatever reason/purpose God allowed the sign/coincidence to occur; it has brought him glory, and that's great.

But sometimes, misinterpretation may lead you away from God. You just happen to run into an ex-girlfriend outside the grocery store for instance. You get to talking and you get back together . . . when it was an ungodly relationship and you knew God didn't really want you to be together. Have you really listened to the Holy Spirit of God warning you against taking the coincidental meeting the wrong way and subsequently is getting back together with her edifying to God? Or is it merely edifying to you and your sinful nature?

For if it's merely for you and your so-called glory/power/ego . . . then have you interpreted the coincidence in a Godly way? You have listened to yourself then, rather than the Holy Spirit.

Indeed your need to learn that lesson in practice may be part of why a negative result may eventuate from what you initially but inaccurately saw as a positive sign of God's guidance.

So while God's providence may occur through means of a coincidental meeting . . . so too do many ungodly temptations and backsliding possibilities also occur.

The trick is to keep discerning and being humble and receptive to what God would have you do . . . rather than just what you might like to do. As a result, you need to contain your eagerness to interpret the event as a positive so-called 'sign' of God's favor/attempt to guide you. It might very well not be that.

Just because you met coincidentally, doesn't mean God wants you to get back together with your ex. (For just one instance for the purposes of enlightening this discussion surrounding God's providence and coincidence.)

"A man's heart plans his way, But the Lord directs his steps."[13]

While I do see this verse as evidence that God/the Holy Spirit's direction may well be behind many of those coincidental meetings and events in life but it is important to remember that what he wants will come to pass, regardless of the plans you have for yourself. However it is important not to twist this meaning. How does God want you to interpret the events that come to pass? Not just how do you want to interpret these events . . .

As a former counselor, I'm all for the foundational paradigm of Narrative Therapy; where the counselor helps the counseled re-define the narrative in their story to discover the hidden strengths, and both the larger and smaller story taking place in their life.[14] As a result, keeping in mind the big picture as well as the fine details; how does God want you to react and tell the stories of your life to others? Would he like you to twist many of the signs/images you're bombarded with on a daily basis into making him the sole arbiter of the direction you've chosen in life? Making him responsible for your choices? Does that seem responsible? Wise?

And yes, God directed my steps on my journey to the writing on the wall. And that's great that I can see it and praise him for his intervention. For a long time, I think I twisted this meaning into believing that I was

13. New King James Version, *Proverbs 16:9*, www.bible.com
14. White, *Narrative Therapy*

special because God had intervened in so obvious a way. That was not however I believe how God wanted me to interpret and react to the writing on the wall.

I believe how he wanted me to react was to be grateful, humble and to simply share about my experience here with others, so they too would see it and praise God and have even more faith in him, than they had before they heard about my experience. And for a long time, I didn't share about this event. I didn't apply Luke 8:39 to go and tell of what God had done for me.[15] I felt people wouldn't understand. There are so many fine details that make his intervention and guidance amazing here and I felt it would be hard to communicate about it effectively and accurately. People are also busy and just want the short story, summated in the synopsis of course. And I like to share the short version a lot these days, simply to bolster people's faith in God and many do marvel, like I do still, at his gracious intervention.

Still, I thank you, the unseen reader for your willingness to read the full story and sit with me as I analyze all these events in order for you to better understand what I did well in interpreting the spirit's voice and what I still need to do better. For much of the 'advice' I give to you; don't think I'm excluding myself as someone who always does this… I need to follow it too! And I hope you are encouraged and have a better understanding of what it takes to effectively discern the Holy Spirit speaking to you as well as the nature of the Holy Spirit's guidance from reading this book. This guidance is through God's providence of not just his internal direction in us but also making us more aware of his intervention in all your various external circumstances in life; whether they are as a result of intentional actions on your/his part or just seemingly somewhat coincidental.

But please please please don't twist your interpretation of signs and coincidences into saying you can avoid personal responsibility for your resultant choices. To say; "It's God's fault, I'm here. Not mine."

Ezekiel 18:20 says "The child will not share the guilt of the parent, nor will the parent share the guilt of the child."[16] We are each responsible for our own attitudes . . . and attempting to shift blame onto God for our potentially misguided interpretations that labelled us each interpreting a sign as coming from God . . . when it did not or if it did, resulted only in our sin; won't expiate us from our responsibility to discern wisely the various signs/coincidences we are confronted with in life and act appropriately.

15. New International Version, *Luke 8:39*, www.bible.com
16. New International Version, *Ezekiel 18:20*, www.bible.com

God didn't buy Eve's excuse that it was the snake's influence that caused her to sin.[17] And he won't buy yours . . . even if you try to tell him that it was merely from a sign he brought into your life that resulted in your misinterpretation and consequentially, your sin. He hasn't bought my excuses either.

17. New International Version, *Genesis 3:13–16*, www.bible.com

Conclusion

Living Dangerously with the Holy Spirit

"My people are destroyed for lack of knowledge."[1] — Hosea 4:6

PRIORITISE GOD

And now to the conclusion of the matter at hand.

I began the journey to the writing on the wall in obedience and faith . . . but still had doubts (and that's ok) as to whether the impression/voice in my head, was actually the voice of God . . . I finished the journey at the writing on the wall in full knowledge that that voice had indeed come from both outside/inside myself and was therefore, God/the Holy Spirit.

Hence this book details an effective experiential rebuttal to those who would argue the Holy Spirit is merely an illusion.

In addition to leading me to greater holiness, I believe the Holy Spirit is capable of predicting the future and guiding my steps with or without my conscious knowledge; and has shown me an amazing instant prediction and immediate unlikely in human terms (considering the "odds" of it happening), fulfillment.

Because I've experienced this firsthand, I declare that I no longer have a child-like simple faith in God. Faith in the sense I am speaking here, implies accepting something on 'trust' — without proof to some people. According to such an idea; I no longer have faith . . . I have experienced "proof" resulting in the "knowledge" of God's existence and of his Holy Spirit living inside me and speaking directly to me. Sometimes with using

---

1. New King James Version, *Hosea 4:6*, www.bible.com

thoughts of actual words inside my mind. (Though I still very much have to accept Jesus' faith journey in the Bible, on faith, as being the reason for the hope that I have . . . [2] I was not alive when he was crucified after all and did not "see" that particular "proof".) And because of this knowledge, I have felt a responsibility to pass along my journey and my knowledge to you. "To he who has been given much, much will be asked"[3]; and "Why do you call me Lord, Lord and do not do what I say?"[4] So, I am doing it Lord! I am living this. In the words of Isaiah, "Here I am Lord, send me."[5]

And everything in the Bible, in Jesus' journey, about living by faith, with the Holy Spirit; that speaks about such things, I fully believe and I believe my own journey to Christchurch as detailed here backs this up; when one dares to listen to the Holy Spirit in practice. As well as providing living proof in practice of this verse:

"This is the covenant I will make with them after that time, says the Lord. I will put my laws in their hearts, and I will write them on their minds."[67]

There is nothing contradictory I have said in this entire book with fundamental, conservative, Christian doctrine/interpretation or application that I am encouraging here. I may be a charismatic worshipper in church but I am not pentecostal; largely because I believe some of their holy spirit and prosperity doctrine to be inherently flawed and as such is easily twisted.

Jesus and many apostles/saints 'wonderful plan for prosperity' that God had for them . . . was to largely suffer brutal deaths and many forms of financial poverty for instance despite their largely complete obedience and faith being put into practice.

I also believe, to all who truly believe/repent; God has poured out the 'counselor'[8] the Holy Spirit to live and guide each of us, within us.[9] We all have it in equal measure . . . but we all do not listen to the holy spirit in equal measure, nor are God's plans for any two people, the same, so the

2. New International Version, *1 Peter 3:15*, www.bible.com

3. New International Version, *Luke 12:48*, www.bible.com

4. New International Version, *Luke 6:46*, www.bible.com

5. New International Version, *Isaiah 6:8*, www.bible.com

6. New International Version, *Jeremiah 31:33*, www.bible.com

7. New International Version, *Hebrews 10:16*, www.bible.com

8. Revised Standard Version, *John 15:26*, www.bible.com

9. New International Version, *Joel 2:28*, www.bible.com

Holy Spirit gives different instructions to different people. Nor are any two people who are justified, in the same way, ever in the same place of sanctification in their walk with the Lord.

What I will say, is that if you desire the knowledge of God . . . and so, not to be destroyed as in the verse quoted at the beginning of the conclusion from Hosea[10], you too must learn to prioritize, listen to, and obey the Holy Spirit living in you as well as get to know God's character better by reading/meditating on his word. And if you are doing all these things, great, I pray that God blesses your own tests with him, like he chose to bless me through my tests with him.

Also, you may experience failure on your 'road' way to success with God . . . but God's guarantee I believe is "I will not fail you in the way that matters." God may not directly answer or guide you in as clearly an obvious/vindicating way as he did with me on my journey . . . but one answer you will definitely get . . . is to learn to trust him more and to value that more. It is also not easy to trust someone you don't know. So just as I've allowed you to get to know me in this book; I will emphasize again . . . And I can't say it enough. Get to know God. Read the Bible. Cover to cover. Though if you're a new christian, I would suggest starting in Matthew. Each book reveals different aspects of God's character. And the Bible is a living word . . . each time you re-read a passage; depending on where you're at in life and what you're going through; the Holy Spirit *may* illumine it differently for you as if you're reading it for the first time. To consider both; "what does this verse mean to me," and "what does this verse mean at the time/in context." Taking both; not just either; into consideration is a genuine path of wisdom I feel.

I trust God so much more than I did after I found the writing on the wall — though to even find that I believe I have shown that my trust in him was much greater than many dare to show in action.

To be honest, it was a relief to feel vindicated in the journey at the writing on the wall . . . that it hadn't simply been "me" leading "me" — that it had in fact been God leading me.

This leads me to comment on a song lyric by Steve Camp and Rob Frazier (from 1989): "Living Dangerously in the Hands of God" from Steve Camp's beloved album "Justice". Which I have pasted some of this lengthy lyric below, for immediate reference/comments on after.

---

10. New King James Version, *Hosea 4:6*, www.bible.com

How easily Jesus is forgotten
Amid the comfort of my life
How the flames become a flicker
And faith a brilliant disguise . . .

. . . Oh, to gladly risk it all
Oh, to be faithful to His call
Abandoned to grace
But anchored in His love
Living dangerously in the hands of God . . .

. . . So let me live like I believe it
And though my faith is prone to fail
Though I cower under trial
By His grace, I shall prevail

There's safety in complacency
But God is calling us out
Of our comfort zone into a life
Of complete surrender to the cross
To live dangerously
Is not to live recklessly but righteously
And it is because of God's radical grace for us
That we can risk living a life
Of radical obedience for Him

You've got to walk on
For the Lord, He walks with us
You've got to walk on
Oh, though it costs you everything
You've got to pray on

For the eyes of the Lord
Move to and fro throughout the earth
That He may strongly support those
Whose hearts are completely His . . . [11]

11. Camp, *Living Dangerously in the Hands of God*

BE DARING

I dared to live dangerously, with a radical obedience to God's strange call to leave my house and travel to Christchurch . . . seemingly on a whim but I was 99 percent sure it was the Holy Spirit leading me there.

I was open to hearing God . . . and obeying him . . . regardless of the consequences — and not afraid to have mud on my face if the journey turned out to be merely led by me (and I was 99 percent wrong) and not the Holy Spirit. Whilst always employing 'holy' behavior on the journey, I wasn't out to hurt anyone or myself. Just listen to God; hear what he had to say, see what he wanted me to see and importantly, submit fully to God and do what he wanted me to do.

To live "dangerously is not to live recklessly (though some decisions may seem reckless to others) but righteously."[12] (In the sense of what righteousness in practice is; seeking the Lord with pure motives and being fully open to him, holding nothing back in your commitment to him.)

God's grace is radical . . . and sometimes, so too is the calling of what the Holy Spirit may ask you to do . . . But there is no sin in it as there was no sin in my radical obedience to travel to NZ (though as explained in the chapter confession time, I nevertheless remain a sinner; albeit a repentant one who seeks God's glory) though it may appear foolish in the eyes of mankind to simply drop everything on a whim in order to simply "come and follow" Jesus[13] when I felt that call come.

I also recognize, I am making a radical statement on what is required/obedience to God here/listening to the Holy Spirit. God calls us for *full commitment!* Those who are lukewarm, as I again indirectly quote the Bible; will be spat out of his mouth![14]

As the lyric also says "There's safety in complacency . . . but God is calling us out of our comfort zone into a life of complete surrender to the cross."[15]

I completely surrendered in my journeys to return the apple to the tree and the writing on the wall. It wasn't easy. Those particular journeys still seem wild and crazy to me . . . And as stated elsewhere, I still resist the Holy Spirit, in small ways, daily. No one, (other than Jesus) in their life on

---

12. Camp, *Living Dangerously in the Hands of God*
13. New International Version, *Matthew 4:19*, www.bible.com
14. New International Version, *Revelation 3:15–16*, www.bible.com
15. Camp, *Living Dangerously in the Hands of God*

earth, will ever be able to live a fully complete life of complete surrender to the Holy Spirit.

But, as you learn to trust the Holy Spirit inside you; a little more each day . . . your faith will grow as will your knowledge of him as will his blessings upon you and even through you, to others.

And I pray that this, and perseverance is what ensues for you. So, that you "inherit the crown of life"[16] and are not destroyed for "lack of knowledge" of God.[17]

REDEFINING BLESSINGS

I would now like to make a short comment on the erroneous belief that success is material and that any forms of either man or god defined success, rests solely on our abilities.

God led me to success in finding the writing on the wall. It certainly didn't rest/rely on my abilities but on his guidance and ability. If it had rested solely on me, I would have inevitably found the back door of a different house unlocked; with no writing on the wall, and no permission to stay there.

And only found 'failure' instead of vindication/success.

So, in listening to the Holy Spirit; I would like you to redefine blessing and success in the terms of how/what God defines success as. Which I will summate as the point of the journey of sanctification. "Holiness". And pleasing God.

"And without faith it is impossible to please God, because anyone who comes to him must believe that he exists and that he rewards those who earnestly seek him."[18]

He rewarded me for my faith by giving me direct knowledge/experience of his existence and proving to me that it was indeed his Holy Spirit who was guiding me when he led me to the writing on the wall.

That is the greatest *blessing* of all. God himself.

Money, Family, Career, Popularity, Power, Possessions. Such things can be as much a sign of God washing his hands of you (Being fed up with you!) and giving you over to your sin-filled passions[19] as they are "bless-

---

16. New International Version, *James 1:12*, www.bible.com
17. New King James Version, *Hosea 4:6*, www.bible.com
18. New International Version, *Hebrews 11:6*, www.bible.com
19. New International Version, *Romans 1:24*, www.bible.com

ings." If you actually use those things as blessings for his kingdom, rather than to merely build your own ego of course — then maybe those *blessings* aren't a sign of God wiping his hands of you and simply giving you as an immature child[20] exactly what you want regardless of whether you should be given those *blessings*.

As of course, poverty, trials, sufferings . . . can also actually be redefined as a form of blessing; given, perhaps, because of your prior unwillingness to trust him, prioritize him and listen to the Holy Spirit . . . because as trials, they are *possibly* meant from him to draw you into a greater wisdom and reliance on him. Will you learn what he wants you to know from them? Will you rely on him? Or will you curse him even more for sending things you don't like your way? I don't like that he hasn't sent me a Godly Wife thus far . . . I don't like that I pretty much live in poverty according to western standards of affluence . . . But I accept what God gives and takes away . . . [21] because I trust him. Knowing the writing on the wall . . . I cannot live any other way but trust him completely . . . even as some things, some days I hate . . . and other days I love.

To repeat the words of Job: " . . . the Lord gave and the Lord has taken away; may the name of the Lord be praised."[22]

REDEFINING SIGHT

I released a short film last year (available on my youtube link at the end of the conclusion) about the influence the Holy Spirit has on you called "The Clown"[23] and featured in it, the first verse of Amazing Grace quoted below:

Amazing Grace
How sweet the sound
That saved a wretch like me
I once was lost but now I'm found.
Was blind but now I see.[24]

Even though I didn't think I was; I was blind to the Holy Spirit influencing my mind before returning the apple to the tree and since the writing

20. New International Version, *1 Corinthians 13:11*, www.bible.com
21. New King James Version, *Job 2:10*, www.bible.com
22. New International Version, *Job 1:21*, www.bible.com
23. Wallace, *The Clown*
24. Newton, *Amazing Grace*

on the wall, I cannot help but see him and hear him everywhere and in everything; from the personal influence he's had speaking inside me and proving his words to me. I truly was blind . . . and now, I truly see. I sing those words with gusto! And I praise God for his marvelous grace in saving a wretch like me.

Many are those who've read those words, even sung them and yet remain blind, unable to see the Holy Spirit attempting to speak to them. Unable to discern his presence inside them and refusing every attempt by the spirit to lead them. Writing it off as "rubbish." They aren't open to hearing God's Holy Spirit speaking inside. But you all have God's Holy Spirit inside . . . please . . . if you do nothing else this year, I pray you open yourself up to that still small voice . . . and start to listen and hear, test if need be and ultimately follow the promptings of God's spirit in whatever form those promptings may take. He doesn't want to lead you astray. You are already astray.[25] He wants you to be found. He wants you to see what I've seen. Now go, find your own writing on the wall. Whatever that may be for you. And wherever that path may lead; though it be "through many toils, dangers and snares. Twas Grace that brought me safe thus far . . . "[26] (see my life-test for proof of that! By "man's standards" I should be dead) "And Grace (God's unmerited favor on my life who I praise out of sheer gratefulness for what he has done for me!) will lead me home."[27]

Now I pray you trust the Holy Spirit as I do, if you do not do this already of course.

So having shared what I wanted to share in this book, I also feel ready now to answer Tim's recent question to me of why now, Justin? Why write/ share this book now and why come back to Gateway Baptist, 18 years after you left. For starters, I never wanted to leave. I was happy there. It was the Holy Spirit who led me away after returning the apple to the tree… and begrudgingly, I left; obedient to the Holy Spirit's call. And then for months after I returned to Greenslopes, I felt the call to return there, but I ignored it… petulantly… focusing instead on women and the things I shared in the Confession Time chapter that needed to be overcome. My stumbling blocks. And as I overcame them, with a fresh start in a new place that helped, I overcame my own disobedience and returned to Gateway.

25. New International Version, *Romans 3:23*, www.bible.com

26. Newton, *Amazing Grace*

27. Newton, *Amazing Grace*

In my heart, I knew the way forward… months before even moving to Greenslopes and a long time before writing this book had ever even occurred to me. So, as part of doing that, when I hurt my back in 2022 in a previous job; I looked for a job/financial means of added support that would require me to move away from my 'rut'. And when I got the job at the Hospital I'm still in as I type this; I moved closer to it; gleeful. A fresh start. And it was only when I realized I had overcome my stumbling blocks and that I wanted to share this full story with someone who had gone from strength to strength in the years since my friendship with him had faded; that I decided to write this book. That what I had to say and share, had merit; not really for Tim who didn't need it but who might be interested in the full story of course; but for all those people who would see value in what I had to say and share about my journey of learning to trust in God and his miracles that he had shown me in finding the writing on the wall; being proof of God's presence in my mind. Using actual 'word thoughts' even at times. Guiding me. Helping me. Maturing me. Despite at times, my best efforts not to grow in wisdom… And then sharing the wisdom I've learned from my experiences here.

Now, to repeat myself one last time, I've done in this book what the demon possessed man did in Luke 8.

"'Return home and tell how much God has done for you.' So the man went away and told all over town how much Jesus had done for him."[28]

But I'm not going to let it end there. I want to literally go all over town and share my story. I will sell this book in so doing… but its not the book sales that matter to me… It's the opportunity to share my incredible proof of God in my Writing on the Wall testimony and help other seekers find the God they are looking for.

So, now, I thank you, the reader, for reading about my journey as I move forward to this next stage of sharing my calling, I'm going to quote one of my favorite songs, Margaret Becker's Immigrant's Daughter as capturing the heart of my motivation; " . . . falling down on my knees, a calling comes to me . . . I'm gonna run to the land of the living and take everyone that I can with me!"[29]

As for you, moving forward now; I hope what I've said here inspires you to trust the Holy Spirit more as well as, most importantly, leads you to read the Bible more and get to know God's character . . . to help you

28. New International Version, *Luke 8:39*, www.bible.com
29. Becker, *Immigrant's Daughter*

better discern between your thoughts and the promptings of the Holy Spirit speaking inside you.

If you aren't yet a christian, I hope this book encourages you to realize that you live in a broader world where there is an explanation for the seemingly inexplicable and that that explanation is that God undoubtedly exists (How else could I have encountered the writing on the wall? The odds of that are extreme!) and through the Holy Spirit prompting both believers and where necessary, unbelievers (for God's greater purposes) is partly how he chooses to work in the world.[30] I hope you are encouraged to read the Bible more — so that at least your own supposedly "imaginary" conversations with him might stand a chance of having his dialogue in your head be remotely accurate.

If you are a christian, I hope this book has encouraged you to test and place more faith and trust in the Holy Spirit inside you and to allow his spirit to guide you on your own path and choices that yet lie before you each day; whether in larger matters or merely in the fine detail of the mundane as you too journey on your own path of sanctification with the Lord and become more Christ-like, each necessary step of the way. Whether those steps are a joy to take at the time of taking them or whether they are full of pain or confusion. Mostly, for you, I pray for receptivity and humble obedience to the Holy Spirit. Which many times, is the harder, narrow path to walk.[31] It takes courage to walk it. So "be strong and courageous."[32]

There is one final category of reader, I'd like to address my final thoughts to. And that is the person who as a result of reading my story here has been "shocked into faith"[33] as my NKJV study Bible's notes puts it.

My story is confronting and if you think you now believe in God, through recognizing the Holy Spirit inside you, I would encourage you to continue in your journey of faith. Read the Bible, seek out a church or Godly associates to have discussions with; and start to form your own opinions about what you believe and maybe even what in time you think you may need to repent about. Belief in God, always comes first. Then through his spirit, you'll get to know his character and learn which attitudes of yours need to be altered/repented of in order; not to be "saved" from God's wrath/ to be given eternal life; that is through faith in him and through what Jesus

30. New International Version, *Romans 8:28*, www.bible.com

31. New International Version, *Matthew 7:13*, www.bible.com

32. New International Version, *Joshua 1:6*, www.bible.com

33. Sproul, The Reformation Study Bible New King James Version, *2396*

did and by repenting of whatever you currently consider your sin to be; but in order to progress further down the path of sanctification and fulfill in the process your desire to please God simply out of gratitude for his amazing grace that he has extended to you as a sinner. For "God demonstrates his own love for us in this: While we were still sinners, Christ died for us."[34]

There are a million different opinions on a million different issues. It isn't actually that important when you first come to faith to have firm thoughts and opinions on all the issues in life. In time, as you journey with the Holy Spirit; you'll learn what you think. Some things won't need altering. Other attitudes you may grow in wisdom and think something different tomorrow to what you think today. Make up your mind not to allow others or even your own views which you think you may disagree with some Christians on, to become stumbling blocks to your faith in God.[35]

Repentance, like sanctification is an ongoing process. Romans 14 and Galatians 5 are really good chapters on christian liberty/opinion differences; essentially where one person may feel something is permissible/not sin and someone else feels the same thing is sin.[36][37] Each person must be true to their own conscience and give an account to God.[38]

As for that accounting . . . "And what does the Lord require of you? To act justly and to love mercy and to walk humbly with your God."[39]

If this book has influenced you to believe in the Holy Spirit; then I have done my job. But please don't let it 'end' there. Pass my book on to a friend or around members of your Bible study or University Class; get them to read it (or even buy a friend a copy if they're not good people to lend to . . . ;) lol!) Discuss the Holy Spirit and my journey with them. And if you wish to support what I do in any way, please like my facebook writer page to stay up to date about any other developments in my writing career or with this book. If possible, I'd also love to come visit your university, church, Bible study or function to share the short version of my testimony that proves the Holy Spirit exists and messaging me there, may make that happen. Please message me your stories of how God has proved himself to you at my facebook page too for potential inclusion in my next book.

34. New International Version, *Romans 5:8*, www.bible.com

35. New International Version, *Romans 14:13*, www.bible.com

36. New International Version, *Galatians 5:1–26*, www.bible.com

37. New International Version, *Romans 14:1–23*, www.bible.com

38. New International Version, *Romans 14:12*, www.bible.com

39. New International Version, *Micah 6:8*, www.bible.com

In the meantime, I also pray God's blessings, lessons and grace will flow freely on all of you regardless of your perspective, through you to others and upon all you do, think or say.

To God be the glory.

In Jesus name,

Amen.

Justin Brent Wallace

MBus, BA, Dip Teach, Dip Couns.

Writer (At the Urging of the Holy Spirit)

"The Writing of the Wall — Seeing the Holy Spirit in Life"

www.justinbrentwallace.com

www.facebook.com — Search "Justin Brent Wallace - Writer"

https://www.youtube.com/@JustinWallace-ue4fd or @ AnonymouseMovies

As well as

Writer/Director/Editor/Producer

"Immortality" — Feature Film — Anonymouse Productions

Greenslopes Queensland Australia

www.facebook.com/anonymouseproductions

Outside Australia:

www.amazon.com : (keyword search "Immortality Paul Tucker")

In Australia:

https://vimeo.com/ondemand/immortalitymovie/414145281

Interested in booking Justin to share his miracle testimony in person for free of his "Writing on the Wall" experience at your school, college, university, church, camp or bible study group? Please direct message him after searching "Justin Brent Wallace - Writer" on his Facebook page to help make that happen.

Afterword

A Second Conclusion

"We've had one yes, but what about second breakfast?"[1]
— The Lord of the Rings

What's this? A second concluding chapter? As a huge Lord of the Rings fan, no book of mine would be complete without at least one quote from it and now we've had it! I can tick that off on the bucket list. For now that I've had this book contracted to be published, I thought, given that this story is largely a memoir... that I'd finish with a second conclusion from a cute short memoir story/analysis of an event that just happened to me in the present on February 16, 2024 and not some 17 years earlier.

You see tonight I re-watched one of my favorite films as a cat lover; "A Streetcat named Bob" and I was struck by a number of similarities between James/Bob's journey and mine/Terry's journey thus far.

Struck, like I mean, struck by the Holy Spirit struck too.

There I was, all emotional in the closing credits; feeling joy that James achieved success in his life with Bob a key part by his side[2] and hoping very much I achieve the same; and even if that is not forthcoming for me, I still identify with James' journey to a lesser degree (my addictions are obviously different and to a much smaller effect than his were of course) and I listened to the lyric of a song being sung by the actor who played him in the film and the line "I fell in the river and got pulled down"[3], really struck me.

---

1. Jackson, *The Fellowship of the Ring*
2. Spottiswoode, *A Street Cat Named Bob*
3. Fink, *Second Time Around*

Obviously I literally fell in the river that night I returned the apple to the tree and soon, metaphorically, got pulled down into a well intentioned but sinful lifestyle in pursuit of finding God in life. Which coincidentally (!) happened to be the next line. "I had good intentions but I lost my way"[4].

Which I did in that journey beyond until very recently.

And my last lesson from that, which I'm very happy to share is that taking responsibility for the care of a rescue/shelter cat like Terry a few years ago really, gradually, helped me learn greater responsibility in life… and also, as a result, begin to look back at my past experiences and learn how to better share about them… feeling more responsibility now to make the most of the gift God gave me in proving that he used actual words in my mind to communicate with me and proved his existence to me hence, when he led me to the writing on the wall.

I've also learned a thing or two spiritually from taking care of my cat about God's relationship with us. You see in this analogy, we are the cats… like Terry who looks longingly most days out the screen door at the birds and desires to pounce on them. But as his loving, benevolent master like God is with us, I know that outside it is dangerous for him. I cannot let him roam fully free and know in my heart that he is being well taken care of. I live near a major street and if Terry got out, there is a large chance he'd get hit by a car. There are also sadly some street tough alley cats nearby; who I wish I could help . . . but first things first. Yet if I opened the door; in Terry's instincts he'd lunge for those birds and chase them. He wouldn't think twice. So as much as its up to him to learn how to quieten those instincts and settle for a longer, happier life with me in the ways that matter . . . It's also up to me to guide him and protect him from danger. And that is God's role with his lost sheep. He brings them back into the fold and merely asks us to accept that his yoke is easy and his burden is light[5]; knowing that the pathway to true lasting, as opposed to temporary happiness is found only in so accepting such a light yoke from God in turning away from your sin; and not killing the birds . . .

Yes, I've applied a song lyric heard to events from my life . . . But it is the Holy Spirit who helps me see the relevance to my life and learn lessons from it. This final example is yet one more way I see the Holy Spirit in life everywhere I look. And I hope from reading this, you're now even more open and aware of how to truly see the Holy Spirit in life too and be

4. Fink, *Second Time Around*
5. New International Version, *Matthew 11:30*, www.bible.com

more inspired each day by God's majestic tapestry of how he amazingly weaves all things together for the good of those who love him, who have been called according to his purpose.[6]

6. New International Version, *Romans 8:28*, www.bible.com

My Response to Issues Raised by the Experts

"For we walk by faith, not by sight."[1] — 2 Corinthians 5:7

INTRODUCTION

I now present my response to a number of experts main issues with my book when they were approached for a potential academic comment/review or endorsement of my content to be published with this book. Some, unsurprisingly, refused to endorse and raised, summated below, a variety of the 8 main issues listed why. After stating these issues, written from my point of view; I reveal my opinion and response to each. Please note; some made partially detailed comments—depending on the strength of their feelings regarding each of the challenging issues listed below but no one had all these issues . . . Different people/experts had different numbers of the below issues to differing extents.

1. Interventionist God.

2. Total Commitment to God.

3. A Need for God's Grace.

4. Influence on Weak Minds.

5. Foundational Challenge to Christian Counseling Methodology

6. Foundational Challenge to Secular Psychiatry/Psychology Methodology

7. Liberal Holy Spirit Interpretation of Life's Stimuli

8. I set an example of a Potentially Dangerous Denial of Established Mental Health Diagnoses

1. New King James Version, 2 Corinthians 5:7, www.bible.com

1. Interventionist God

I show unarguably an Interventionist God in existence (who clearly inter-vened for me in showing me the writing on the wall)—some people believe in a God who doesn't intervene . . . who created and sits back . . . others believe in no God . . . that all is random chance . . . Some simply don't believe in miracles. My journey undoubtedly presents a strong, uncom-fortable challenge to all such viewpoints and those who sit comfortably in what they have always believed. Some also use the existence of some of the below issues in their minds to 'shoot the messenger'; and hence discredit what I say and so have yet another excuse not to believe in God; despite the evidence on the table that my book reveals.

2. Total Commitment to God

My total commitment/obeying and a cavalier attitude as a result to tasks completed under the so-called auspices of the Holy Spirit . . . This idea presents a massive challenge to those of a lukewarm nature who don't have the same level of commitment in their faith to God . . . My journey shines a massive light on their potential lukewarmness as being a strong potential reason why they maybe aren't experiencing the same interventionist God in practice; that I experience in practice and prove that in my book with what happens to me...

3. A Need for God's Grace

I display a strong need for God's grace and intervention to have had to occur to me to be able to write about all this—despite my obvious sin in a number of events detailed that caused me to be put into dangerous situa-tions. Did I unacceptably put the Lord to the test in a way that sets a bad example? Some think so. I think; that even if I did—that just shows God's grace even more . . . and I point to him and his sovereignty that much more than myself in deciding the outcome of what events occurred—even your reading of this book.

4. Influence on 'Weak' Minds

This book may present a possible negative influence on those with 'weak' minds who may be inclined to follow every urge of the Holy Spirit as they see it; and put themselves into dangerous situations in the future—believing God intervened for me—he will surely intervene for them . . . I've done what I can in the text at times to urge caution and appropriate 'testing' of the Holy Spirit's guidance to you/your life . . . I can't be held responsible for every loony who wants to twist what I say to suit them . . . Just as the bible is often twisted by every loony to say something that it actually doesn't say.

5. Foundational Challenge to Christian Counseling Methodology

This book challenges general Christian Mental Health Counseling Practices—to see/acknowledge the Holy Spirit may be involved in some way in some of what their 'client' is telling them or they have experienced . . . To take this into account and not simply dismiss their 'spiritual ramblings of God influencing them' as 'crazy/insane' or even put a simple dismissive label on it as potentially 'demonic'—when God's will may in fact be at play and occurring.

6. Foundational Challenge to Secular Psychiatry/Psychology Methodology

Likewise I present a similar throwing down of the gauntlet—challenge—to Secular mental health practices—which can't explain away how "God" intervened in my circumstances—and I attempt to get them to admit that their model of psychiatric treatment is flawed; as in it's very foundation it refuses to acknowledge the existence even of potential spiritual influences on the behavior of their 'clients' in various events that have unfolded or in the stories of what their clients are sharing with them. It is an insufficient limited model in practice despite its general widespread acceptance by the medical community and used in the secular mental health practice and this affects community expectations. And my book; by connotation and inference, attacks this model/attitude as being insufficient and short-sighted and incapable of explaining effectively what happened to me; and why; and their simplistic diagnostic boxes are hence insufficient and inaccurate and need to be altered as well. And so do by connotation secular general community expectations of mental health treatment as well. Which is also under attack and shown to be a part of the problem by inference/connotation in my work.

7. Liberal Holy Spirit Interpretation of Life's Stimuli

All this is also summed up in a simplistic—"I have a cavalier attitude to interpreting the bible's statements regarding "The Holy Spirit" and resultant willingness to see/hear the Holy Spirit in all of life's various stimuli. This is applied/interpreted as very liberal Holy Spirit theology in practice by those unable or unwilling (hence the challenge) to do this as well as quite pinpoint just how uncomfortable they are at the idea of doing this themselves and even reading about my journey and me daring to do this in practice and resultant logical results and conclusions. No one wants to change or feel uncomfortable. But then; once upon a time; before my journeys detailed here; I too would have strongly disagreed with me and towed a much more conservative, society endorsing line. Now however, I have experienced what I have—and so—as a result of this I must, as Leonardo Da Vinci essentially says in my quote at the beginning of the book . . . change my attitudes/behavior when presented with undeniable proof that refuted clearly what I conservatively once believed—making me I recognize, somewhat of a radical in this area—even though I remain quite conservative in the vast majority of the rest of my theology/practice/life elsewhere.

8. I set an example of a Potentially Dangerous Denial of Unwell Mental Health Diagnoses

Some had a problem with my example/arguments in the book of me being in denial of stated established Mental Health Boxes/Diagnoses . . . You see; in a sense in writing what I have and using this book—this makes me set a so-called dangerous example of a voice for those other voiceless who are also misdiagnosed and mis-treated by psychiatrists, Christian counselors and society who because of their presuppositions pre-judge that 'some' clients presenting with mental health symptoms are unwell—when they might not in fact be unwell; they are potentially merely being obedient to the holy spirit's urging for them to take action in various ways in their life. I give a voice to the unnumbered voiceless others of this idea who may also feel the same way yet can't communicate as eloquently as I can in the publishing stage of the world. These other voiceless clients by connotation that I also represent are also potentially misunderstood . . . as I was . . . mistreated and not hence; helped as effectively as they could have been had their treating mental physicians had a methodology that better took into serious consideration the Holy Spirit's existence and what God might be attempting to say to their client or to say to the counsellor in their treatment through the client's relating and unfolding of their events and presenting circumstances. I make no apologies for this. This forms a key part of my book and reason for writing.

Conclusion

Even though I know my example/words upsets the comfort zone of 'outsiders' and 'treating physicians'. To shake up numbers 5 and 6 above in particular . . . industries that need a shake up from the Holy Spirit as I see it—and I think this is part of the reason why God even chose to intervene in my circumstances as it was . . . to one day be able to write such a book about the Holy Spirit's Potentially Sovereign Influence over events/people that could actually stand a chance of shaking up 'the establishment' and cause enough of a stir to hopefully upset their applecart and may one day result in improved methodological practice across these fields in the future. My book states/proves The Holy Spirit exists and so, should not be ignored . . . In doing so; your actions are NOT as wise as you think they are or they should in fact be . . . Man's wisdom is indeed flawed . . . God's wisdom isn't . . . and he delights to show that what man may consider foolish . . . eg. many of my actions . . . he actually considers wise and dared to endorse my actions by intervening to begin with . . . To prove that this is what happened to me in my book as I state an iron clad case of this also presents a massive challenge to those set in their ways and prejudices that is difficult to accept. Overall, I know my book presents a very tough pill to swallow! Understandably many are resistant to this. Regardless of whether they're from a mental health, theological christian or non-christian or interested community member 'seeking' greater perspective on the possible influence of the Holy Spirit in life.

About the Author

Justin lives with his beloved cat Terry in Brisbane, Australia. He has written a number of screenplays, including one which has been distributed on Amazon Prime Worldwide "Immortality" in 2020 and another which won best unmade screenplay and fan favorite at a U.S. International Christian Film Festival in 2021. Justin has written an as yet unpublished fantasy epic in the mould of *The Lord of the Rings* as well as an as yet un-produced Christian Musical using the songs of Amy Grant and Michael W. Smith. When he is not writing or making films, he can be found on the tennis court and also enjoys a good partner dance in various styles. He has several degrees and previous experience as an English and Drama Teacher as well as a Counsellor.

Interested in booking Justin to share his miracle testimony in person for free of his "Writing on the Wall" experience at your church, camp or bible study group? Please message him after searching "Justin Brent Wallace—Writer" on his Facebook page.

To simply show your support, please like or follow this page on Facebook.

Justin also welcomes direct messages there from people interested in sharing their stories of faith in God being vindicated by some form of proof as he continues work on his next book "Modern Day Miracles: Short Stories of Faith in God vindicated by proof!"

Bibliography

Note: All quotes and references used in this book fall within the category of "fair use" except the lyric reprinted with permission of Steve Camp's "Living Dangerously in the Hands of God"—details on copyright page. Also, all direct and indirect biblical quotes/references in the text and footnotes used are available by inputting the name of the relevant translation, book, the chapter and specific verse into the main search field available on the home page of www.bible.com.

Author Unknown, *What is the Walk to Emmaus?*, https://www.gotquestions.org/Walk-to-Emmaus.html

Becker, Margaret, and Peacock, Charlie, "Immigrant's Daughter", track 1 on Margaret Becker, *Immigrant's Daughter*, Capitol Music Group, 1989.

Camp, Steve and Frazier, Rob, "Living Dangerously in the Hands of God", track 4 on Steve Camp, *Justice*, Capitol Music Group, 1989.

"Crazy", MP3 audio, track 2 on Gnarls Barkley, *St Elsewhere*, Warner Bros, 2006.

Dindal, Mark, dir. *The Emperor's New Groove*. 2000; South Yarra, VIC, Australia, Buena Vista Entertainment, Disney, 2001. DVD Disc, SD.

Fink, Charlie "Second Time Around", Original Song from *A Streetcat named Bob*, Sony Pictures, 2016.

Homer, *Odyssey*, Lattimore, R (Translator), *The Odyssey of Homer*, Harper Perennial Modern Classics Reissue Edition, New York City, New York, 2007.

Jackson, Peter, dir. *The Fellowship of the Ring*. 2001; New Line; Sydney, NSW: Roadshow, Sydney, 2002. DVD Disc, SD.

Kipling, Rudyard, *If* (Poem) as part of *Rewards and Fairies (1st ed.)* Macmillan, London, 1910.

Marquand, Richard, dir. *Return of the Jedi*. 1983; Moore Park, NSW: 20th Century Fox, 2006. DVD Disc, SD.

Newell, Mike, dir. *Harry Potter and the Goblet of Fire*. 2005; Neutral Bay, NSW; Warner Bros, 2006. DVD Disc, SD.

Newton, John, "Amazing Grace", printed as part of *Hymnal*, Edwin Othello Excell, Chicago, ILL, 1909.

"Not by Sight", MP3 audio, track 6 on Petra, *Not Of This World*, Star Song/A&M, 1983.

Reiner, Rob, dir. When Harry Met Sally. 1989; Beverley Hills, CA: Castlerock Entertainment, Polygram Entertainment, 1998. DVD, SD.

Sinach, "Way Maker", track 1 on Sinach, *Way Maker*, Mayolee, 2016.

Sommers, Stephen, dir. *The Mummy Returns*. 2001; Universal City, CA: Universal Studios, 2001. DVD, SD.

Spottiswoode, Roger, dir. *A Street Cat Named Bob*. 2016; Universal Sony Pictures, 2017. BLU-RAY, HD.

Sproul, R.C. (ed), *The Reformation Study Bible New King James Version*, Sanford, FL; Reformation Trust, 2016.

Toms, Garry, *God's Love Language Sermon*, Greenslopes Baptist Church, Greenslopes, QLD, Australia, 24th December, 2023.

"Too Many Times", MP3 audio, track 4 on Michael W. Smith, *Project*, Reunion, 1983.

Turteltaub, John, dir. *National Treasure*; Burbank, CA, Disney, 2004.

Wallace, Justin, *Facebook Friend (Name withheld) News Feed Post Martin Luther Meme*, 23rd December 2023, https://www.facebook.com.

———, *Facebook Friend (Name withheld) News Feed Post Paul Washer Meme*, 24th December 2023, https:/www.facebook.com.

———, dir. *Immortality*. 2016; Burbank, CA, Adler and Associates Entertainment, 2020.

———, dir. *The Clown*. 2022; Greenslopes, QLD, Australia, https://www.youtube.com/@JustinWallace-ue4fd, Anonymouse Productions, 2023.

Wimpenny, Stephanie, *Facebook News Feed Post Permission Detail Screenshot*, 12th January 2024, https://www.facebook.com.

White Michael, *Narrative therapy with children and their families*, Dulwich Centre, www.dulwichcentre.com.au. 2006.

Yates, David, dir. *Harry Potter and the Half-Blood Prince*. 2008; Neutral Bay, NSW; Warner Bros, 2009. DVD Disc, SD.

www.ingramcontent.com/pod-product-compliance
Lightning Source LLC
Chambersburg PA
CBHW071803090426
42737CB00012B/1926